Tributes from the Press

MBE

Editorial Comments
on the Life and Work of
Mary Baker Eddy

Tributes from the Press

Editorial Comments on the Life and Work of Mary Baker Eddy

Discoverer and Founder of Christian Science, and
Author of the Christian Science textbook,
Science and Health with Key to the Scriptures

The Christian Science Publishing Society

Boston, Massachusetts, U.S.A.

Editorial Comments on the Life and Work of
Mary Baker Eddy

© 1911, renewed 1938

The Christian Science Publishing Society

Tributes from the Press: Editorial Comments on the Life
and Work of Mary Baker Eddy

New Material © 1993

The Christian Science Publishing Society

ISBN: 0-87510-233-6

Library of Congress Catalog Card Number: 92-75488

Printed in the United States of America

Designed by Joyce C. Weston

Introduction: Twentieth-Century Biographers Series

IN THE closing years of the twentieth century, there is a growing awareness that the hundred years since 1900 will have registered a magnitude and pace of change, in every aspect of human affairs, which probably exceeds any historic precedent. In political, social and religious institutions and attitudes, in the sciences and industry, in the arts, in how we communicate with each other, humanity has traveled light years in this century.

"Earth's actors," said the Founder of Christian Science, Mary Baker Eddy, "change earth's scenes. . . ." As we look back over the landscape of this century, some towering figures emerge into view: political leaders, scientists and inventors, authors, artists and musicians, social and religious pioneers, industrialists, and many others who helped "change earth's scenes."

Mary Baker Eddy is regarded as a major religious figure of the twentieth century and as a notable example of the emergence of women in significant leadership roles. Although her book *Science and Health with Key to the Scriptures* was published in 1875, in 1992 it was recognized by the Women's National Book Association as one of 75 major books by women whose words have changed the world.

Mrs. Eddy's works are visible today in virtually every country of the world: in church buildings, in Christian Science Reading Rooms, in the distribution of the newspaper and religious periodicals she established and their derivative broadcast forms, in the wide circulation of her own writings, and most important, in the way hundreds of thousands of people conduct their everyday lives.

Mrs. Eddy wrote only briefly about herself, in a short volume titled *Retrospection and Introspection.* She discouraged personal adulation or attention, clearly hoping that people would find her character and purpose in her own writings rather than in the biographic record. Yet, she came to see the need for an accurate account of her life and gave specific if possibly reluctant acquiescence in the year 1910 to the publishing of the first of the biographies — Sybil Wilbur's *Mary Baker Eddy.*

As we near the close of a century which directly witnessed some of Mary Baker Eddy's major contributions, The Christian Science Publishing Society, the publishing arm of the church she established, has reexamined the church's obligations to future generations and centuries, in providing an appreciation and understanding of her remarkable career. The Publishing Society now welcomes the opportunity of publishing, and keeping in print, a major shelf of works on Mary Baker Eddy under the general series title: "Twentieth-Century Biographers Series."

Mrs. Eddy's career and works have stirred humanity in the twentieth century and will continue to do so. Perhaps an appropriate introduction for this series is captured in her statement, in the Preface to *Science and Health with Key to the Scriptures:* "The time for thinkers has come." In that spirit, this series of biographies by many different twentieth-century writers is offered to all those who, now and in the future, want to know more about this remarkable woman, her life, and her work.

Preface

THE COMMENTS in this small book were originally compiled by The Christian Science Publishing Society in 1911, the year following the passing of Mary Baker Eddy. They were excerpted from personal tributes, special articles, and editorials appearing in newspapers and magazines. Immediately after Mrs. Eddy's passing, the *Christian Science Sentinel* printed six pages of comments from more than thirty publications. So much material was written, however, that it was decided to issue *Editorial Comments on the Life and Work of Mary Baker Eddy* the next year. In the introduction to the original book, the Publishing Society said: "It is believed. . . that the articles and excerpts herein presented are indicative of a general desire to render honor where honor is due, and that the book will be welcomed not only by Christian Scientists but by fair-minded thinkers everywhere." *Editorial Comments* was reissued in 1923 with some modifications.

Tributes from the Press: Editorial Comments on the Life and Work of Mary Baker Eddy contains virtually all of the 1911 text, the 1923 modifications, and new introductory material developed for this publication as part of the

"Twentieth-Century Biographers Series." This volume is being published because of its historic place in the Publishing Society's record of the life of Mary Baker Eddy.

It contains four articles written by editors of the religious periodicals — two by Archibald McLellan, who at the time was both a Director of The Mother Church and Editor-in-Chief of the periodicals, and two by Annie M. Knott, who was an Associate Editor. Besides these articles by Christian Scientists, there are approximately 175 other pieces, many of which are excerpts from longer articles or editorials. Many were still referring to Christian Science as either a cult or a sect, but the choice of these words was not meant to be pejorative. Some confused Christian Science with optimism, but this was because the writers saw the outward manifestation of Christian Science in its students. The *Chicago Post* described Mrs. Eddy's followers in terms that we would wish emulated in every generation:

> Without humbug or sentimentalism, any outsider can and must admit that Christian Science people are good people. They not only believe in their church and attend its meetings with a passionate faithfulness that other churches envy, but they also carry their faith with them into their daily lives. By its very nature they have to. For

if Christian Science means anything to any man or woman, it must mean everything.

Today's reader may not decide to read all these pieces at one sitting. Many of them cover similar territory in the nature of their comments. What is more interesting, from the perspective of a better part of the century that has passed since 1910, are precisely those aspects which are emphasized by their repetition. The sheer magnitude of the growth of Christian Science impressed even those who had no particular interest in the religion. With some exaggeration regarding the number of Christian Scientists, the *Calgary Herald* commented:

With the death of Mary Baker Eddy, one of the most remarkable figures of this or any age passes from the world's stage. To have been for half a century the head of a great movement is a lot conferred on few. To have been for the same length of time the center of heated controversies, of bitter attacks, of religious and philosophical arguments, is a record that few would have survived. To die at the age of ninety, leaving a devoted following that numbers millions of souls, with their churches scattered throughout the world, is but the climax of a wonderful career.

Somewhat more soberly, the *Chicago Tribune* wrote:

She has builded in her own lifetime a great religious institution, a faith widespread and held by hundreds of thousands of believers. And not only is the number of her following notable, but likewise its character.

Others commented on the fact that there were by 1910 more than one thousand Christian Science churches, or that the growth of Christian Science had been viewed as a challenge by most other evangelical churches, or on the good citizenship and harmonious dispositions of Christian Scientists in the community.

For those living in an era when Christian Science is not growing everywhere, but where its presence has been well accepted for as long as anyone remembers, it may come as a surprise to know the degree to which the Christian Science movement had already come of age during the last decade of Mrs. Eddy's own lifetime. This awareness, in turn, may lead Christian Scientists to ponder what were the special qualities of thought that characterized the growth of the movement by the year 1910, including this statement Mrs. Eddy made many years earlier to one of the pioneer teachers of Christian Science in Chicago:

Oh may love bind you all in its silken cords. For Truth and Love's dear sake we must be living examples of Unity if that *is* our *Principle* and then the world will acknowledge the power and genuineness of Christian Science.

Richard A. Nenneman
Lincoln, Massachusetts, August 1992

Publisher's Note:
Tributes from the Press: Editorial Comments on the Life and Work of Mary Baker Eddy incorporates modern spelling of place names, as well as the current state abbreviations as designated by the United States Postal Service. In addition, the Index has been similarly updated.

Mary Baker Eddy

Editorial from *Christian Science Sentinel*

THERE IS a story of a certain old-world philosopher who, when it was asked of him, "What constitutes achievement?" answered, "To be able to reply Yes, every evening, to yourself, when you ask, 'Have I done good to any one to-day?' " It would be difficult to find a more practical and efficacious test of the value of a man's life-work, and it would impossible to find any one to whom it could be more fearlessly applied than Mrs. Eddy. Her whole life, even before she discovered Christian Science, constituted an expression of an intense tenderness for suffering humanity, and as the years added themselves to years, and she learned more and more of divine Life, Truth, and Love, she came to fulfil absolutely the exhortation of Paul to the church at Colosse, "Walk worthy of the Lord unto all pleasing, being fruitful in every good work, and increasing in the knowledge of God."

Building in this way for God and not for herself, she built on sure foundations. The Christian Science church which, in the brief space of forty-four years, has literally folded itself around the globe, is in this way founded upon a rock, the rock of divine service. It is a rock against which the storms may beat in vain, for as long as the thoughts of men are turned away from selfish aims, in the endeavor to be able to say, at every close of day, "I have striven to bring healing to the sick, peace to the weary, joy to the sorrowing," they will be learning something of the meaning of consecration.

The depth of man's consideration may be measured by his understanding of divine service. "The song of Christian Science," Mrs. Eddy writes, "is 'Work — work — work — watch and pray'" (*Message to The Mother Church for 1900,* p. 2), and certainly no one has ever put exhortation into practice with more selfless devotion than has she. "I saw before me," she writes on page 226 of *Science and Health,* alluding to her earlier trials, "the awful conflict, the Red Sea and the wilderness; but I pressed on through faith in God, trusting Truth, the strong deliverer, to guide me into the land of Christian Science, where fetters fall and the rights of man are fully known and acknowledged." Not once, in all those years of conflict, did she flinch, because not once in all those years did she put her own will before the will of God; and so to-day the Red Sea and the wilderness lie far behind, and the advancing hosts of Christian Science hear the voice of their Leader, repeating the triumphant words of her Master, "Fear not, little flock."

What Mrs. Eddy has won for Christian Science, her followers will maintain and increase, because she has given them a scientific understanding of Love; and, as she herself says, "Where shall the gaze rest but in the unsearching realm of Mind? We must look where we would walk, and we must act as possessing all power from Him in whom we have our being" (*Science and Health,* p. 264). Though they stumble and falter as they press forward, press forward they must, because they have realized that the demands of divine Science are imperative, and that the peace of God which they one and all seek can only come to them in proportion to the measure of their performance.

This performance has, however, to be something more than individual, it has to be collective as well. Even in the affairs of this world the proverb declares that in union is strength. If this is true of the effort of discordant minds and temperaments to achieve a human victory, how much more true must it be of that unity in the service of God which is founded on unity of thought and action. Such unity is to be wrought out only in the determination to seek another's good rather than our own, for self-seeking is the seed which would grow into the tree of disintegration.

This is the lesson which Mrs. Eddy has held persistently before her followers, and we can only claim to be her followers in proportion to our obedience to her teaching; and to obey that teaching we have to devote our efforts to the attempt to live in good. "Who lives in good," she writes, on page 4 of *Pulpit and Press,* "lives also in God, — lives in all Life, through all space. His is an individual kingdom, his diadem a crown of crowns. His existence is deathless, forever unfolding its eternal Principle. Wait patiently on illimitable Love, the lord and giver of Life. *Reflect this Life,* and with it cometh the full power of being. 'They shall be abundantly satisfied with the fatness of Thy house.'"

Archibald McLellan

Onward and Upward

Editorial from *Christian Science Sentinel*

Christian Scientists the world over have another reminder that they must arouse themselves as never before to prove by demonstration the priceless teachings of their beloved Leader. This she has always urged them to do, but the human tendency often leads us to rely upon another to work out our problems for us, and so far as this is yielded to we lay needless burdens upon others, and miss temporarily the unfoldment of our own spiritual capacities.

Some years ago, when Mrs. Eddy found it necessary to go away from Boston in order to gain greater freedom for the revision of *Science and Health,* and also for the writing of other books which have so wonderfully enriched our literature, many of her followers were greatly disappointed, because, as it then seemed, their captain had retired from the field and left them to fight their battles alone. Soon, however, they learned that this was far from being the case. As a result of the greater freedom gained by seclusion, she was enabled to work out the rules for our church organization, The Mother Church and its rapidly increasing branches, as given in the *Manual*. She also provided for the establishment of the Lesson-Sermons, Christian Science reading-rooms, the board of lectureship, the committees on publication, and the extension of our literature in the publication of the *Sentinel, Der Herold,* and the *Monitor*. The *Journal* had been established by her in 1883, and she continued to be a frequent contributor to its pages.

Among the many other achievements of Mrs. Eddy's years of retirement from society, may be reckoned the building of The Mother Church edifice in 1894, also its magnificent extension in 1904, and later the erection of the publishing house. All of this, however, is but the outward expression of the mighty Christianizing influence which had its present-day inception in the giving to the world of *Science and Health with Key to the Scriptures*. The redemption of thousands upon thousands of professed Christians from a doubting and uncertain faith in God and the promises of Christ Jesus, and the awakening of vast numbers of avowed agnostics to a vital faith in these and a new-found love for God and man; the physical healing of multitudes and their moral and spiritual quickening, — these are the things that really tell the story of what she attempted and by the grace of God accomplished. Well may the lesson of her life arouse all her followers from the lethargy of mortal belief and the delusions of mere personal ambition, to wholehearted service in the cause of Truth.

The cause of Christian Science is firmly established, thanks to Mrs. Eddy's reflection of divine wisdom and her unceasing toil. To us is now committed the glorious task of seeing to it that no smallest portion of our spiritual heritage shall be lost to posterity, because of any lack of appreciation or energy on our part. As we think of our beloved Leader, crowned with a record of long and selfless service such as the world has seldom seen, we may recall Tennyson's characterization of a great English statesman, —

Whose eighty winters freeze with one rebuke
All great self-seekers trampling on the right.

Mrs. Eddy's followers are such because most of them had hungered for but failed to find that which her teaching offers, the Science which reveals the facts of being, including man's limitless possibilities as a child of God, and which makes all the promises of Christ Jesus an absolute certainty. Like the Samaritans who listened to their townswoman's story of Jesus' wonderful teachings, we can say, "Now we believe, not because of thy saying: for we have heard him ourselves, and know that this is indeed the Christ, the Saviour of the world." Jesus, as a personal teacher, left his followers, but he promised that the Comforter, "the Spirit of truth," should come and abide with them forever, should bring to their remembrance all that he had taught them.

Mrs. Eddy has ever directed her followers to look away from her personality to the Holy Comforter, and as they have striven to obey they have found the eternal and infinite source of all comfort, the Life divine. They will prove their love for their divinely inspired Leader by greater faithfulness at every step of the way; they will "wait upon the Lord" and "renew their strength;" they will "run, and not be weary; . . . walk, and not faint."

Annie M. Knott

"Judge Righteous Judgment"

Editorial from *Christian Science Sentinel*

It seems only fitting at this time to devote a large portion of our space in this issue of the *Sentinel* to excerpts from the columns upon columns of editorial comment that have appeared in the secular press during the past week, — a tribute in its apprehension and appreciation of the greatness of our beloved Leader and the work she has done for humanity at large, as generous as it is wide-spread.

There is one phase of this comment which is characteristic. Few of the editorial writers lay claim to a personal knowledge of the teachings of Christian Science, but with very few exceptions they concede that its Discoverer and Founder was a wonderful woman and that she wrought a wonderful work; that the world is better and happier because of her, and that wherever this faith has become established its exponents are "living epistles" that make for the general uplift of the community.

It is true that Christian Scientists do not need to be told how truly great is the mission of Christian Science and how much of good it has accomplished. None know better than they the tireless energy, the unfailing watchfulness over its welfare that in the last forty years has gone to its establishment and upbuilding; that there was no fear or faltering on the part of the Leader who set her hand to the fulfilment of her high calling, but it is none the less gratifying when such generous tribute to the greatness of her accomplishment is paid by those who have judged her by the Scriptural standard: "By their fruits ye shall know them."

One can but ponder, however, how much more of good would be accomplished if the teachings of Christian Science were more generally accorded recognition, if the truth it presents in all its beauty and simplicity, the truth which centuries ago Christ Jesus declared should make men free, should lead them out of the darkness of despair into "the glorious liberty of the children of God," should be accepted in its entirety. One can but believe that the ever lessening minority of those who misjudge and condemn Christian Science do so because they have failed to apprehend, to lay hold on its animating and dominating truth, that because God is omnipotent good, evil is shorn of its assumed power; that the reasonableness of its propositions lies in the fact that they are demonstrable by each and every one in the proportion that they are accepted and put into practice.

In this connection a clipping from the *Washington* (D.C.) *Herald,* which reports a sermon by one of the pastors of that city, is particularly apropos. The Rev. Lloyd Douglass, preaching from that wonderful promise of the Master which is the foundation stone of Christian Science practice, — "He that believeth on me, the works that I do shall he do also; and greater works than these shall he do," — said:

I am not a Christian Scientist, and my position as pastor of an orthodox church makes that point quite clear. Yet I had rather be identified with that cult than to be identified with the large and increasing body of people who are zealous in impugning all of its teachings without going to the trouble of investigating.

When Mrs. Eddy began her teachings she felt the Christian church was failing to realize the practical value and usefulness of the power which Jesus Christ had delegated to his disciples. Some of the most ardent enemies of Christian Science are people who have not taken the time or trouble to study the principles set forth in Science and Health. It would be better if these people would devote their controversial powers to some matter upon which they had more information.

We read in the Gospel of Luke that when Jesus came back to his home town of Nazareth after his experience in the wilderness, he read in the synagogue this prophecy from the book of Isaiah: "The Spirit of the Lord is upon me, because he hath anointed me to preach the gospel to the poor; he hath sent me to heal the brokenhearted, to

preach deliverance to the captives, and recovering of sight
to the blind, to set at liberty them that are bruised." Here
in epitome is the mission of Christian Science, the work in-
augurated by our Leader and its every obligation fulfilled,
— the work it is the high privilege of Christian Scientists
everywhere to carry on in faithful continuance, watching,
working, and praying until the light which has come to
them through her teachings shall "radiate and glow into
noontide glory" (*Science and Health,* p. 367); until the leav-
en shall have leavened the whole lump, until men everywhere shall see in Christian Science the undivided gar-
ment of Christ Jesus.

Archibald McLellan

A Tribute

Reprinted from *The Christian Science Monitor*

It is the testimony of Holy Writ that love is stronger than
death, and at this hour Christian Scientists are proving the
truth of the inspired saying. Their beloved and revered
Leader, Mary Baker Eddy, has left the earthly scene of her
untiring activity in the service of God and humanity, and
in the solemn hush which follows their human sense of
loss they realize as never before the depths of their love for
this noble and true-hearted woman whose life of devotion

to Truth has meant so much to unnumbered thousands of lives that were in deepest darkness until the light of Christian Science dawned upon them. Poorly indeed would they prove their understanding of her teachings did they at this hour yield to any unreasoning sense of sorrow. Mrs. Eddy has ever insisted that God, not man, is "the centre and circumference of being," the Principle and Life of all, and to this eternal fact they will cling until the goal of spiritual being is reached, and the deathless life proved by Christ Jesus is attained. Mrs. Eddy's discovery of the healing and saving power of divine Truth was brought to a densely materialistic age, but in spite of this it has aroused mankind to lay hold upon all that the Bible promises. To-day, after nearly half a century of arduous and unselfish toil on her part, the Scriptures are a mighty, life-giving power to multitudes who before the coming of Christian Science knew them only as the letter that killeth.

With the temperament of a seer, Mrs. Eddy has always chosen to be alone with God in pondering the solution of the great problems of being, and as a result of her communings with the Mind that governs the universe she has shown the utmost wisdom in directing the activities of the rapidly extending Christian Science movement, its success being due to her wonderful ability so to present the truth as to inspire those about her with something of her own faith in God and her sublime courage in working for the triumph of good over evil in every phase of human experience. Her followers can now do no less than defend the heritage of truth which she has left them, until it sets all men free.

Mrs. Eddy has glorified the teachings of Christ Jesus in making them a living power to-day as truly as nineteen hundred years ago, and to her belong his words of commendation: "Well done, good and faithful servant . . . enter thou into the joy of thy Lord."

Mrs. Annie M. Knott

Excerpts from
Editorial Comments

The Woman's National Daily, St. Louis, MO

IT IS peculiarly human to venerate and sanctify our ancestors and stone those who seek to better life while we are living it. But a comparatively few years ago a man died whose life had been spent in causing the world to swim in blood and misery. The world trembled and gasped in relief as he died, and then proceeded to glorify him as it had groveled at his feet while he lived. He had emptied a million homes of their breadwinners, caused more widespread misery and distress than any man who ever lived, and built a world empire which crumbled before he was gone; yet when Napoleon Bonaparte died all the world bowed its head in tribute to the beating he had given it.

Two nights ago a frail little old gentlewoman died who, too, had built an empire, but not of blood and misery. A million hearts silently mourned her for a moment, but in accordance with her own teachings it was only a tribute of love and loyalty for the brighter, better view-point of their own life and death she had taught them. There was no pomp; but a few brief words following the usual services, and the announcement that a loved and revered Leader had exchanged a mortal form for an immortal one. She had shed no blood, destroyed no homes, shackled no nation, but what she had done was to take away a little human misery and substitute a happier, better attitude toward life. She taught nothing new, for what she taught was but a different view of the first thing — the beginning and the end. We may differ from that view, but none even now can doubt but that she was one of the most remarkable souls that has appeared in human guise.

We cannot know how much of such rare human lives is abnormal genius and how much a message and a lesson put in understandable, humanly tangible form by divine Love. Certainly, whether we agree with teachings or reject them, the lesson is the same and the world grows better with each such lesson. We stoned her for a time, as usual, and perhaps she will be soon forgotten, or perhaps future generations will cloak her with divinity. At any rate, the world owes that frail woman a greater debt than it owed the world-conqueror, and if her works be of life they will live; and if not, they will die, but the fact that even a single life has been made better will not be lost in the world's melting-pot from which through countless centuries a great purpose, beyond our human understanding, is being worked out. Some time in the future, perhaps, the race will stone the bloody monster who seeks to make it swim in blood to gratify his own lust, and honor the pure of heart, who seeks to brighten it; but we are not yet quite that civilized. I have never read Mrs. Eddy's book or teachings, but I have seen some results of them which compelled both honor and respect, and I believe that all are agreed that a reasonable way of judging a tree is by its fruit. Nothing could have been finer than the way of her going and its reception by the multitude whose Leader and loved teacher she has been.

Chicago Tribune

With the death of Mrs. Mary Baker Eddy there passes from this world's activities one of the most remarkable women of her time. Whatever the degree of faith or unfaith with which the individual may look upon what she taught and what was accomplished by or through her teachings and her influence, the amazing and well-nigh miraculous achievement set down to her account cannot but impress the imagination and arouse our profound consideration. She has builded in her own lifetime a great religious institution, a faith wide-spread and held by hundreds of thousands of believers. And not only is the number of her following notable, but likewise its character. Mrs. Eddy has not swept into her church myriads of the unthinking and uneducated. On the contrary, her teachings have appealed to the highest classes, and the level of the character and intelligence of the Christian Scientists is everywhere high.

As to the right value of Mrs. Eddy's message, the permanence, importance, and extent of the church she founded, no contemporary estimate or prediction is worth much. A hundred years from now it will be easier and safer to evaluate her teachings, the worth of the work she did, and her own place among the men and women who have risen to lead and influence powerfully and extensively the lives, the thought, and the spirit of their fellow-men.

Boston Globe

The deep sorrow felt by Christian Scientists over the loss of their Leader, Mary Baker Eddy, will be shared by people of broad sympathies outside that church who regret the passing of any notable figure. The impulse toward higher standards of conduct in life which had its birth within her mind will continue to live and influence humanity.

Within a generation Mrs. Eddy founded and established a sect, and lived to see her teachings accepted by many people scattered throughout the entire world. The ethical part of her faith, pointing to rules for every-day conduct, has found general favor, and it is chiefly the therapeutic side of her teachings that has aroused criticism. Whatever one's view on religion may be, few will care to deny that Mrs. Eddy's influence has been directed toward the betterment of those that she intimately touched. It must have been singularly gratifying in the closing days of her life to realize how widely her belief has been adopted, for few men and still fewer women live, as did Mrs. Eddy, to see their fullest hopes realized. This is not an appropriate time to set an estimate upon her right to enduring fame, which can better be judged by posterity, but the present-day testimony must be one of respect for a woman of remarkable mind and of unusual ability, who, after a long and active life, spent her closing years at peace with the world. She has now passed on, leaving behind her an institution that she created.

Concord Monitor, NH

Whether one agrees or disagrees with the Christian Science faith in its concept and practice, few, we think, will deny to the Founder of that church the laurels of greatness and the right to be called "a wonderful woman."

Study the story of her life as written by friend or foe, — the impartial pose toward her seems to have been a very

difficult one to maintain,—and every careful and thoughtful reader must be impressed with what Mrs. Eddy accomplished in her old age, for the dawning of her success was
not much more than twenty-five years ago and she was
eighty-nine when she died. The permanence or brevity of
the spiritual empire she created, the extent of her influence
upon modern thought and life, will be justly valued soon
by time, the great appraiser. Whatever that verdict may be,
the memory of Mrs. Mary Baker Eddy will long be cherished in Concord, the city which by her and through her
has been so much beautified and benefited.

Boston Post

The passing of Mary Baker Eddy removes one who for
more than a generation past has been a force of exceptional
magnitude in the spiritual life of a large following. The
cult which she introduced, and of which she remained the
acknowledged and venerated head and exponent to the
very end of her long life, has in it elements which have appealed strongly to many people.

The record of the Christian Science church is phenomenal in the history of modern religious movements. It is
hardly thirty years since The Mother Church was organized here in Boston, and today its branches number more

than one thousand and its congregations are established in the eastern as well as the western hemisphere. This has followed the quiet, persistent spread of those ideas of which Mrs. Eddy stands as the author. It is not necessary that one should hold agreement with the postulates of Christian Science to recognize this marvelous extension of the cult and to appreciate the fact that Mrs. Eddy has exercised a tremendous power in directing it. She pointed out the applications, as she conceived them, of religious ideas nineteen centuries old, in their relation to the conditions of life among the people of today.

As was to be expected from the range of the doctrines propounded by Mrs. Eddy, strong antagonisms were aroused, and it is in meeting them with steady calmness that she demonstrated the stability of her own personal faith and gave inspiration to those who accepted her leadership and stood with her. Even those in emphatic disagreement with Mrs. Eddy's doctrines may well recognize in her a remarkable personality.

New York American

So wide-spread is the fame of Mary Baker Eddy that there is no country in the world that will not take note of her death. Her extraordinary influence upon her generation will everywhere suggest comparisons or contrasts between her work and that of the seer who died in Russia a few days ago. Count Tolstoi spoke to the intellect and Mrs. Eddy to the heart. Nobody has any right to doubt the sincerity of either; though every one will think and feel as he pleases or as he can — concerning their wisdom and inspiration.

Thousands of homes in America and elsewhere have felt the cheer of her brave spirit — and will cherish her memory with the feeling that it is a reviving and inspiring presence. But no reflective person can doubt the significance of the great rally of the human mind against the discouraging materialism of the nineteenth century — a revolt of the soul against mechanism and fate, in which this woman played so remarkable a part.

New York Morning Sun

The creed which Mrs. Eddy built in the minds or hearts of her multitude of disciples has one aspect or incident which seems to us to deserve universal recognition. It is apart from any question concerning the theology, the pathology, the psychology of her doctrines, and apart even from the facts of her personal career.

We are thinking of the astonishing influence she exerted in thousands of homes for the amelioration of life and manners in some of the details of family and social inter-course. She taught cheerfulness of spirit, and observation encourages the belief that the great majority of her follow-ers either became more cheerful, both subjectively and as consistent examples to those around them, or with more or less success simulated a modification of temperament in that respect, which amounts in practice to nearly the same thing. She taught charity in judging the deeds and motives of another — who does not know of more than one case in his own circle of acquaintance where apparently hopeless vinegar has become oil because of her? She went so far as to devise a vocabulary of euphemism, which proceeds in the right direction, no matter how you may regard some of its extreme manifestations; for there are many habitual and conventional asperities of expression which serve beyond doubt no better purpose than to intensify the sentiments they denote.

It may be said that this is nothing more than an insistent application of principles common to all the forms of the Christian faith. Granting that, is it any the less the duty of candor to recognize the effort and results and to acknowl-edge the service?

Morning Telegraph, New York City

It is satisfactory to know that the great work started by Mrs. Mary Baker Eddy, who died last Saturday, will go on. The world owes much to the woman who apparently discovered a great truth, and who at least has raised thousands out of the slough of despond, converted a multitude of hypochondriacs into hopeful and cheerful persons. Mrs. Eddy lived until she was in her ninetieth year and never wavered in her deep-rooted faith, and died affirming it. So thoroughly had she instilled her views into her followers that her work will live after her, and without doubt the Christian Science church will expand, gather in disciples, and continue to do the good work.

Manchester Union, NH

Mary Baker Eddy, who died on Saturday night at a ripe old age, was a woman who had made her mark upon the time in which she lived. It is as idle as it is contemptible to refuse to recognize facts, and the church which she founded is a substantial fact indeed, in whatever light it may be viewed. That a woman at middle life should have gathered about her a little band of pupils and should have so impressed her teachings upon them that they became her devoted disciples, that she should have lived to see that little company increase and expand until it became a religious organization counting nearly a thousand churches and more than eighty-five thousand members in this country alone, and with branches in most of the countries of the world, is a fact which may well attract the interest and hold the attention of any one who desires to be well informed and who professes to hold an open mind.

It is a development which must be admitted to be the more remarkable because it came in a period of the most notable discoveries in medical science. At the same time that the effect of certain germs upon the physical organization was beginning to be understood, Mrs. Eddy and her followers boldly and persistently maintained that disease is more of the mind than of the body. Nor were those followers gathered only from among the ignorant and the credulous. The character of the members of Christian Science churches is such that ridicule may be said to have become itself ridiculous, and it has well-nigh ceased.

❧

Chicago Post

The passing of Mrs. Mary Baker Eddy brings to a close a life story that is one of the most wonderful that this country of unlimited possibilities has to show. Out of nothing that is physical, no great fortune, no industrial invention, no inherited opportunity, Mrs. Eddy built up a great career. It is the greater because its greatness was not for herself but for the church which she founded. She took from the Bible one of the fundamental commands which modern Christianity had overlooked, the solemn injunction to "heal the sick." This, with an inspiration that burned steady and serene for long years, she put into a faith and a creed that has brought happiness and health and the active religious spirit to thousands upon thousands of her fellow-beings.

This accomplishment cannot be denied her, even by those to whom Christian Science is most distasteful. Its proof lies first in the growth and solid strength of the Church of Christ, Scientist, and secondly in the character and bearing of the members of that church. The stately church buildings in this city and its suburbs, and the constant additions to their number, give concrete evidence of this marvelous development. But more significant than the church buildings, more meaningful than the numerical strength of the church, is the character of its congregations. Without humbug or sentimentalism, any outsider can and must admit that Christian Science people are good people. They not only believe in their church and attend its meetings with a passionate faithfulness that other churches envy, but they also carry their faith with them into their daily lives. By its very nature they have to. For if Christian Science means anything to any man or woman, it must mean everything.

It is this inherent strength in the fundamental idea of Mrs. Eddy's church that will hold it together even after her hand has been removed from its direction. The faith will still live. Only by a full realization of this fact can the outside world gain any comprehension of the calm exaltation of spirit with which Christian Scientists will receive the tidings that the earthly career of their Leader has closed. Only in this way can it understand dimly their fine and vivid belief that "there is no death" in the old pagan sense of that solemn word.

Boston Traveler

Mrs. Eddy has been one of the world's greatest benefactors. Her followers will say more than that, perhaps, but there is no reason why even her enemies should say less. Regardless of differences of faith or philosophy, the world must recognize, in her work, a vast contribution to human happiness. Certain it is that Mrs. Eddy found the world full of doubt and despondency, and gave it a larger measure of brightness and hope. She taught the weak that they need not be weak, the sick that they might be well, the suffering

that they had it within themselves to end their wretchedness. Those who were ailing, physically or mentally, were
enabled, as she herself had been, to become strong in soul
and body. Neurasthenia and melancholy yielded to the
gospel of optimism.

Call it what you will, it is a fact that Christian Scientists,
as a class, are healthy, hopeful, happy, and prosperous. And
Christian Science modes of thought have permeated the
thinking of the world, outside the pale of the church. It is a
great thing to be a teacher when the teaching bears such
fruit. And as Mrs. Eddy, full of years, goes to her rest, the
world is full of gratitude for the good she has done.

Boston Transcript

It is peculiarly characteristic of Massachusetts, so generally
derided as hard-fisted, unsentimental, and ultra-practical,
that here spiritual and emotional ideas take strongest root.
Not ideas and practices that connote spectacular demonstrations, but those that lie close to the fundamentals of life.
This fact has led to the sneer at Boston and Massachusetts
as the home and favorite haunt of fanatics, and such zealots are rather pleased to be so called. The anti-slavery pro-
pagandists delighted in the term. So did the spiritualists,
and we have not known much resentment of it from the

devotees of the cause whose Founder passed on Saturday night. Of all these causes, Christian Science has flourished most and most amazingly. And that growth has come in a period that we are used to calling especially commercialized, narrow, and sordid. Indeed, many persons regard its success as due almost wholly to a natural revulsion or at least reaction from this overmaterialistic public spirit. That may account for its growth, but it can hardly account for its origin, which was certainly due to the genius of one woman.

What a rise and growth it has had! It is the only world religion, so far as we can now remember, that had its rise in an English-speaking country, and is the only new one that has been created for centuries. Wonderful spiritual forces must have been set at work to accomplish this marvelous result. Somewhere in it must be germs of truth. Otherwise its story would be utterly inexplicable. No other recent cause has had such tremendous territorial extent, either in this country or in the world. All these things must be conceded by those to whom Christian Science is utterly enigmatical or anathema. These cannot understand the theory of its application, but they must admit the beneficent results that often come from this treatment and they recognize the satisfaction which Mrs. Eddy had a right to feel over the triumph of her cause. Few founders of a religion have been so rewarded in beholding the tangible success of their labors. Most of these founders died in ignominy and defeat.

Springfield Union, MA

No just or accurate estimate of the character and work of Mary Baker Eddy is possible at this time, and anything that may be attempted in that direction must necessarily fail of the approval of a very considerable number of people. About no personage of her generation has so much and such bitter controversy raged as around the Founder and Leader of the organization and doctrines known as Christian Science, who has just died. The facts of her life and the very question of her existence in recent years, as well as the value of her teachings and example, have been a subject of fierce and acrimonious contention. Many years must elapse before an adequate and fair summing up of her work can be made. But, from whatever view-point one regards the subject, it is beyond the possibility of dispute that she was one of the most influential as well as one of the most remarkable figures of the age.

In the last few years the power and vitality of the Christian Science movement has been shown more clearly than at any previous time. However much Christian Science has been overestimated as a reformative and constructive agent, however strained or unsound some of its tenets may be, it has unquestionably been a force to influence thought and religious institution, and its effect has been felt far beyond the membership of the Christian Science organization. The dignity of her bearing, the patience and self-control she has displayed in the most trying emergencies, have been no slight contribution to the success of her cause. To have preached uniformly the doctrine of peace and love to so many listeners, year after year, is in itself a great thing. In the element referred to as "healing" Mrs. Eddy seems to have touched a spring that is giving religion a new impulse in modern life. How deep and how genuine this really is, must be left to the future to determine.

Lynchburg News, VA

Mrs. Mary Baker Eddy may properly be estimated as one of the most remarkable women of the age. As the Founder of a new religious cult; as the projector of what she believed was the true Science of Christianity; as the builder of a great church with ramifications reaching all over the nation and beyond its borders, she has long stood out as a bright and shining target for the arrows of vituperation, of ridicule, of scorn, of implacable hostility, of the bitterest of cynicism and the harshest of jeers. It was because she survived these things; because the storm and tempest which beat upon her availed not to drive her from the doctrines for which she stood; because amid the stress of almost super-human trial, and the fierce avalanche of opposing arguments, she serenely held safe poise of mind, and fealty to conviction, and fidelity to purpose, that she should be accounted great. Though everything in which she believed and which she taught should hereafter fall and crumble beneath the assaults of logic and research and demonstration; though with her death should also be witnessed the decadence and the early death of Christian Science, — things which we by no means predict, — yet Mrs. Eddy's place in history would be secure as one who achieved to tremendous purpose; who wrought mighty results; who was revered by vast hosts of intelligent, God-fearing men and women and children as the mighty mistress of a cause that was noble in objective and good in inspiration; that accomplished much in affording relief from human ills and the peace of mind for those who craved and needed helpful ministration.

It is not necessary to believe in Mind-healing as Mrs. Eddy believed in it, to accord her this distinction. It is not necessary to give intellectual acceptance to the creed of her church, to concede that Mrs. Eddy nobly lived and worked and aspired — and that she deserves to be ranked among the most striking, the most interesting, and the strongest figures that every graced and distinguished the annals of her sex.

Montreal Star

Mrs. Eddy's death leaves her work, which was that of building up the Christian Science organization, well entrenched, with all the necessary and visible signs of a thoroughly officered going-concern. There are churches in abundance, a great newspaper, bands of devoted adherents, whose "daily walk and conversation" are examples to the best communities in the world. The movement has spread so that its followers may now be found in almost all of the English-speaking countries, and to a lesser extent in the rest of the world. With Mrs. Eddy's disappearance, in all human probability, the course of her followers will vary little, and the cause she espoused will probably suffer no immediate negation.

Atlanta Constitution, GA

One need not be a subscriber to or even a sympathizer with the creed of Christian Science to recognize its Founder,

Mrs. Mary Baker Eddy, as a remarkable and achieving figure of history. Founders of religions and creeds there have been in plenty, but not in our day, at least, has there risen one to build so stanch and so phenomenally an increasing following as that which pays tribute to Mrs. Eddy as its originator and Leader.

When all is said and done, it remains that this woman taught and achieved in large measure that conquest of the flesh by the Spirit that is all too sadly needed in an age engrossed with the lure of substance. She disseminated happiness and cheerfulness among men and women, inspired hopefulness to those that were sick of heart and gave many a battle-weary spirit courage to face once more in the direction of the dawn. By whatever term it be described, that accomplishment stands for the furtherance of good and the encouragement of uplift. And, on the personal side, there are elements of greatness in a woman who could win and so persistently hold the love and absolute confidence of a following mounting into the many thousands.

Inland Herald, Spokane, WA

The death of Mary Baker Eddy removes from earth one of the most remarkable characters of history. In a full and consecrated life of nearly ninety years she accomplished two things, either of which would have crowned her with immortality. The American business man is not only over-worked but overwrought and overworried. His practical training affords him no philosophy. His one need is the se-renity and relaxation of mental rest. He needs a mental an-chorage that at the same time sustains and buoys, but across the anchor which he throws out into the unknown seas must be written "absolute certainty." There must be no questionings.

Christian Science affords its believers just that. Its cardi-nal doctrines of the final supremacy of eternal good and the swift doom of imagined evil are doctrines which, put into practice, confer a calm serenity and unshakable confi-dence that is only good. Christian Science is a practical, in-spiring religion. It was born of a woman, and it has been baptized in the tears of grateful millions. In its promulga-tion Mary Baker Eddy has answered the cry of thousands of tired hearts. In this, if in nothing else, she has been a great benefactor to the world.

Her second great achievement has been the organi-zation of a mighty church in a single lifetime. She ac-complished in one generation that which followed only centuries after every other great religious leader. No other founder of a great church ever lived to see his work com-plete. Neither Confucius, Gautama, or St. Augustine ever beheld the fruit of his teachings materialize as Mary Baker Eddy did. Few will mourn the death of Mary Baker Eddy as other deaths are mourned. Her own doctrines preclude that. Moreover, her personality was something apart, always above and apart, and but little known and understood. But, whatever the verdict of the ages shall be, Mary Baker Eddy to-day sits enthroned in the hearts of thousands and thousands of admiring followers, her remarkable accomplishments an epitome of one of the most extraordinary and potent personalities the world has known.

✳

Butte Evening News, MT

The United States has lost, in the death of Mary Baker Eddy, one of the truly remarkable characters of the century. That in this practical age the beliefs and theories of Mrs. Eddy interested and held nearly a million people sincere and devoted to their Leader, and that this fidelity continued year after year with increasing force, demonstrates not only that Mrs. Eddy was a woman of superior intellect, but that she was one of innate goodness to have stood the test of time. Mrs. Eddy's accomplishment is remarkable in that it was attained without evangelizing or proselyting. Her church might be called a natural growth, and it grew with the dignity which characterized the woman herself. It had chiefly to contend with ridicule of the practical class, whose materialistic natures could not and would not accept the teaching of the woman. Some responsive chord her teaching certainly found in the public mind, and nothing has ever shown that her influence was other than good. Even if Mrs. Eddy accomplished nothing more, she effected in her followers a mental harmony which in this busy land, with its tendencies to discord, was in itself — to those who needed it — a benison.

Mrs. Eddy's disinterestedness stands out prominently. She is free from the accusation of promoting her own worldly affairs at the expense of her zealots. The fruits of her years of labor revert to the organization she planned and perfected. Mrs. Eddy was the most striking example the century has had of the power of repose; hers was not a church militant and her church was the antithesis of that of the evangelical whirling dervish whose creed is as transient as it is tempestuous. From all walks of life, high and low, Mrs. Eddy recruited her army of followers; hers was no appeal to any particular class, nor to any particular nationality, and in point of universality in America the sect was in a class by itself. Few will advance the theory that Mrs. Eddy has not left the world better than she found it.

Kennebec Journal, Augusta, ME

In the death of the Founder of Christian Science, America has lost another of its greatest women. However much we may have disagreed with her or have criticized her utterances, we can but admit her greatness and the remarkable power she had of leading. She founded a religious sect that has shaken the foundations of every evangelical church in the country. Her life has added one more proof that humanity longs for a belief in the spiritual, for trust in a higher power and for visual evidence of its agency. Mrs. Eddy's religion appealed to the sick, the afflicted, and the hypochondriac, where others appealed to the outcast and the forsaken. She won largely, and the force of her character will be felt in her church for all time. Regardless of the merits or demerits of Christian Science, it has become an unmistakable influence of the century. Mrs. Eddy built a church which has drawn to it persons of culture, education, and property, and we have no doubt that it will go on.

Philadelphia Public Ledger

Whatever may be the opinion of the world at large upon the doctrines inculcated by the church of which she was the Founder, it is a question whether Mary Baker Eddy in the building up of this organization of half a million fervently loyal adherents has not outdone the achievement of any other woman who ever lived. There has been many a woman who "led her soul, her cause, her clan" to the accomplishment of a great humanitarian undertaking — who notably contributed to the promotion of temperance, to the amelioration of the lot of slaves or prisoners, to the effectiveness of missionary labor in the domestic or the foreign field, or to the alleviatory ministration to invalids in hospitals in war-time or in times of peace. The world has quite recently been called upon to mourn the passing of two such women — Florence Nightingale and Julia Ward Howe, both of whom were of approximately the age of Mrs. Eddy when they obeyed the summons of the invisible. But Mrs. Eddy was more than philanthropist and humanitarian. To create such a church and to inspire a following so numerous and so devoted, Mrs. Eddy must have been a woman of altogether extraordinary personal endowments.

Denver Times, CO

Mrs. Eddy appeared in an age when men had begun to cast off the outward observance of religious teachings. Success was the fetish men were worshiping. When she first spoke the greater part of the world smiled and shrugged its shoulders. What did a woman know of soul life? But as Joan of Arc led a nation out of bondage, Mrs. Eddy pointed the way to a delectable land of Spirit in which hundreds of thousands have found consolation. We may not agree with the declarations of Mrs. Eddy; we may not be of the opinion that they will be as universally accepted as some of the older religious ideas, but we do think that Mrs. Eddy deserves a high place in the estimation of mankind. Any one who has endeavored to make this earth a more pleasant abiding-place deserves well of his fellow-men. Of late years much mystery enveloped Mrs. Eddy. The charge was made that she had died and that an impostor was parading in her place. However, the world had come to accept the statement made by those closely associated with her, that she was still among the living. The announcement of her death brushes aside all former declarations regarding her material condition.

Hypatia helped rekindle the waning fires of culture; Queen Victoria and other splendid women have builded material empires, but as the world hurried on its endless journey the religious life of the people has been carried unfalteringly by women. And Mrs. Eddy stands as one who has made sweetness and light enter far places.

Rocky Mountain News, Denver, CO

Christian Science is a solace, a support, and an inspiration to hundreds of thousands of human creatures. To them it is more precious than their daily bread. In its comforting power to its followers it is entitled to the world's reverence; and therefore the name of its Founder must claim the world's respect.

Happily Mary Baker Eddy lived long enough to see the sneer give place to admiration. The new religion, or philosophy, or "Science," was compelled to make its stand in a nation much given to scoffing and in an age of free debate. That it has survived and flourished, that its Founder overcame all evil report, must be attributed to the deep spiritual effectiveness of the personality and the absolute answer of the faith to the needs of its devotees. No one now doubts that Mrs. Eddy sincerely believed in her mission to mankind. The fair-minded world acknowledges that she possessed a rare endowment of inward vision and external influence, and that she sought to bless her fellow-beings with her "Science" of absolute health. In that bestowal, her labor was a "marvelous work and a wonder." And through unnumbered generations and by countless millions of devotees she will be revered as the most inspired woman of all time.

There is always a possibility of schism in a church when

it comes to its first loss of leadership. But in the case of the Christian Science cult such division is not now probable. The creed and practice have been settled within well-defined lines; the membership is an intelligent democracy; and not even ambitious or avaricious rivalries would be able to disintegrate the fabric. From the days of popular "exposure" and ridicule, Christian Science has moved quietly and efficiently onward to its present high station. It has brought peace to many tempest-worn lives; it has given health to many pain-racked bodies; it has conferred content upon many tortured minds; it has established faith and cheerfulness, where formerly was despair of this world and doubt of the hereafter. For all the beauty and usefulness which it has given to a million lives, the faith is to be revered and the name of its Founder is to be held in grateful remembrance.

Asheville Citizen, NC

The death of Mrs. Eddy marks the passing of a most remarkable figure in the religious world. Wielding a wonderful influence over a great army, and it was undoubtedly an influence for good, it being reflected in the lives of thousands of her followers, she needed no brass bands to make the world conscious of her presence. While many there are who could not fathom the depths of Mrs. Eddy's teachings, few have denied her sincerity. Her writings bear the imprint of the close student of God and man. Her gospel was largely one of sunshine and mental uplift. Of her home life we know but little, but from all accounts it was an exemplary one.

Mrs. Eddy was also a woman of rare moral courage when we consider that forty years ago she founded a creed at total variance with all established beliefs. The doctrines she enunciated at that time had no other adherent than herself. The scorn and ridicule which greeted her first book has given place to a wide-spread interest, and a great portion of humanity to-day believes that the pill and potion are not essential to the cure of disease.

News Tribune, Duluth, MN

Not Christian Scientists alone, but people of all faiths and no faith, join in tributes to Mrs. Mary Baker Eddy, one of the most remarkable women the world has produced. What the doctrinal teachings of Christian Science are, we do not know; we do not know wherein its interpretation of the Bible differs from that of the evangelical churches. We do not understand the Principle underlying its healing; we cannot, to our own satisfaction, differentiate between the subconscious and the divine Mind. But this is known to all, that Christ gave to his disciples power "to heal all manner of sickness and all manner of disease," and this power was not limited to the twelve.

Moreover, its teachings are accepted, not by cranks and faddists, not by those always seeking something new, but by the educated, the cultured, the thoughtful, and the student. Whatever its secret may be, it has produced a wonderful faith, a marvelous spirit that shows in a power of self-command, of self-denial, of sympathy, and helpfulness that is truly Christian. It has brought a new power into the world, which has gained its way against the fiercest and most stubborn prejudice, against ridicule, scorn, and almost ostracism, until it has compelled recognition and respect, with the acknowledgment of its permanency. To-day, while millions profess open allegiance to Christian Science, many more express a sympathetic interest in it. From a mysterious, sort of uncanny, and somewhat dangerous cult, allied with the black art, to be approached only by those insulated in dread and suspicion, it has taken its place as a faith and as a church.

Mrs. Eddy's dominance has also been resented. She has been misinterpreted, maligned, and persecuted. Volumes have been written against her. Her power as an executive, her administrative ability, and her gift of organization were as wonderful as the faith she founded. Yet that she build her structure on broad, sound, permanent administrative principles, instead of founding a house of cards on shifting sands, has been the cause of most of the attacks personal to her. In this, however, her experience was no different from that of any other great and strong personality in the world's history, and few have left to the world a greater heritage.

Democrat, Johnstown, PA

Whatever may be the judgment of history concerning this remarkable woman and the great organization which she was largely instrumental in building up, this much at least must be said now: Mrs. Eddy has profoundly influenced the lives of many thousands of people, and this influence exerted through the Christian Science church is likely to live long after her frail earthly body shall have moldered into indistinguishable dust.

Times, Louisville, KY

The death of Mrs. Eddy is mourned by a million of her followers. We are too near in time to measure in full the meaning or the value of her work, but the force of her personality and the influence of her teachings have been established permanently beyond all question. No more remarkable woman has been born in this country and none whose work is more certain to live after her. Christians and scientists may differ as to her teachings, but in the minds and hearts of thousands they have won and kept a place and power that have worked mightily in the molding of religious thought.

Milwaukee Daily News

History is full of the tales of women whose influence has been a power in the affairs of men. But, strange as it may seem, by far the greatest number of those who have risen on the written pages of history attained their power through charms of person and through their influence with men of power. But the leading woman of her time, and among the greatest in history, rose to her high place through the power of that which is most eternal in mankind — thought.

Mr. Eddy was not born to power, nor did she seek the influence of those who were so born. By the force of the thought that she expressed and lived has she attained the high place she holds to-day, and by its force will she live. No matter what individuals may think of the system of thought that bears her name, it is an acknowledged power for good among mankind, and thousands have found comfort and relief through its teachings.

Dallas News, TX

To have founded a faith which has its followers wherever there is civilization, and counts them by the hundred thousand, is of itself title to such fame as few men, and fewer women earn. At least this tribute to Mrs. Eddy men of all creeds, as well as the creedless, may unite in giving, for it involves no question as to their agreement with the tenets of the faith which she either revived or instituted. Indeed, it ought to be possible to pay her higher tribute than that without arousing sectarian controversy; for we think it is indisputable that the faith she taught has quickened with hope and joy the souls of multitudes in whom other creeds inspired only a perfunctory morality. Thus it has justified its existence, proved that there was room for it.

Mrs. Eddy and that little band first won by her teaching have suffered the sting of hostile gossip and have often been isolated by a social ostracism, but at least they have not felt the sword nor known the gibbet and the stake; moreover, they have pressed more rapidly than most new creeds did into the circle of toleration. The world at large may still look at them askance, but only in the backwoods are they any longer objects of curiosity. Men are coming rapidly to see that with them at least their faith is real. They exemplify it in their daily conduct with a fidelity that compares favorably at least with the fidelity with which the followers of any other creed manifest their faith; and as men behold it thus exemplified, they have come to see that, instead of being incompatible with Christian morality, it imposes a standard of ethics in which other Christians can find no flaw and conceptions of life beyond the grave that imply the highest degree of religious optimism.

It is this optimism that contrasts so forcibly with some other phases of religious thought which would have us regard this earthly life a vale of tears. From it has sprung that confidence in the unlimited possibilities of the human soul which has literally transformed the physical as well as the spiritual life of thousands of its adherents.

Herald, Washington, D.C.

The death in her ninetieth year of Mrs. Mary Baker Eddy, Founder and Leader of the Christian Science church and system of faith, is an event that will profoundly stir practically every city and community throughout the United States, so universal was the spread of her doctrines and the congregations of her followers. Already from her adherents

have come expressions of regret and outpourings of love —
all of these tinctured with a beautiful faith of the orthodox
Christian kind which allows the believer in the gospel of
Jesus Christ to say over the bier of a beloved one: "She is
not dead, but sleeping."

As to the doctrines of Christian Science which Mrs.
Eddy promulgated with such success, there is still a wide
diversity of opinion, but we think all will agree that there is
much that is inspiring and helpful, even to the most orthodox, in Mrs. Eddy's teachings; and the unprejudiced, those
not of her faith, but of open mind, must in justice admit
that her work, through long years, was always for the betterment and the uplift of mankind.

The religious system she taught was a system of optimism; her promulgations agreed closely with the teachings
and practices of Jesus Christ. She taught the gospel of right
thinking and right living; she taught, in other words and
phrases, the gospel that "a man's work lives after him," and
that, so far, there is no such thing as death. And we shall
find, we think, that her own career will exemplify this
teaching, for though Mrs. Mary Baker Eddy is dead in the
flesh, we know that she shall live in the spirit; that the
work to which she put her hand shall go on, informed always with the soul of love and charity and hopefulness and
faith, to comfort many to whom the old creeds and forms

no longer have appeal. For, without going into the minute particulars of the forms of Christian Science — and of these there are but few — the fact remains that fundamentally the faith of Mrs. Eddy and her followers was the faith of Jesus Christ. It was faith in the eternal goodness of things; the faith that destroys evil and works bravely for the good.

"God is my life" are reputed to be her last written words; words of strong faith that, could they be reechoed by every man, would make the world a happier and better place to live in. Hers was the gospel of salvation by work aided by prayer, and perhaps the one point on which those outside of her church were unable to follow her was in her positive belief in the efficacy of prayer to resolve all human doubts and cure all human ills. But, even in our inability to follow Mrs. Eddy thus far, we are, after all, but confessing that our faith in God's word was less than hers. For it is true, as Tennyson phrased it, that —

> More things are wrought by prayer
> Than this world dreams of. Wherefore, let thy voice
> Rise like a fountain for me night and day.
> For what are men better than sheep or goats
> That nourish a blind life within the brain
> If, knowing God, they lift not hands of prayer

Both for themselves and those who call them friend?
For so the whole round earth is every way
Bound by gold chains about the feet of God.

✠

South Bend News, IN

As the Leader of one of the most remarkable religious movements the world has ever witnessed, Mrs. Eddy found it necessary as well as agreeable to her to live in dignified seclusion, appearing to the followers of her faith at times when the proprieties called for her presence.

Mrs. Eddy's life was notable for its longevity as well as for its purity, beauty, and usefulness. She was born ninety years ago in Bow, New Hampshire, and her youth was spent in sympathetic touch with the picturesque beauty of nature for which the region is famed. Her great grandfather was a man of honored reputation and bore a commission conferred by the provincial assembly. Her father and grandfather were sturdy farmers who fostered in their children the elements of a noble character. The intellectual tastes and assertive strength of her father and the piety and loving winsomeness of her mother were united in her nature, and one who knew her intimately in her girlhood has spoken of her as being distinguished even then for "superior ability and scholarship, her depth and independence of thought, and her spiritual-mindedness," all of which were prophetic of her future work in the world.

The education of the young girl was given careful consideration by her parents, and at sixteen her fertile pen and her ceaseless inquiry and investigation began to disclose that instinct of the poet and truth-seeker which in later years was to achieve such beneficent and far-reaching results. She is said to have been constantly seeking that revelation of truth which would bring her heart assurance and peace, and she followed the path which leads from the plane of common experience to the higher levels of spiritual apprehension. In an hour of hopeless physical suffering she is said to have reached such a realization of the present healing potency of the Master's word that she was immediately made whole. This was in 1866, and since that time Mrs. Eddy has been devoted to the teaching of her faith and its practical application to human needs.

The visible results of Mrs. Eddy's work are found in the establishment of nearly a thousand churches in this and other countries, where the Christian Science faith is taught, and more than a million followers of that faith. Perhaps no religious movement was ever more derided and obstructed in its progress, but it has steadily advanced, and in some particulars, especially in the building of churches without an entailment of indebtedness, has set a new and commendable example.

Birmingham News, AL

In the death of Mrs. Eddy there passes from the stage of life not only one of the most remarkable women that the world has ever seen, but a woman remarkable in a most distinctive way. In the past, women have commanded armies and ruled empires, but Mrs. Eddy was the first of her sex to found a religion, and in this work her greatness lies, not in the line of invention or discovery.

It remained for Mrs. Eddy to assert the absolute nonreality of matter and to pronounce the belief in its existence the source of all evil, both spiritual and physical. And she did this with a bareness, a force and a persistence that won from their former moorings not only minds mystical by nature, but also minds pronouncedly materialistic. It is in this ability to rehabilitate an old thought, swing it clear of long accepted foundation, and drive it home to the consciousness of a materialistic age, that Mrs. Eddy's greatness lies.

Journal-Courier, New Haven, CT

The editorial comments on the life and career of Mrs. Eddy show a gratifying sense of tolerance. Here and there a newspaper expresses its violent dissent from Christian Science doctrines, but the great majority frankly express their admiration of the woman from both a personal point of view and spiritual. Had she died ten years ago this would not have been the case, which is additional tribute to her marvelous power of organization.

It was the *Springfield Republican,* if we are not mistaken, that emphasized the immense good she did in influencing the medical profession by establishing the influence of mind over matter. That truth was not original with her, but it was she who preached it until it became a gospel with over two million souls. The *New York Sun* emphasizes still another phase of her usefulness, and it is this after all that has received such a visible manifestation. Says the *Sun:* "We are thinking of the astonishing influence she exerted in thousands of homes for the amelioration of life and manners in some of the details of family and social inter- course. She taught cheerfulness of spirit, and observation encourages the belief that the great majority of her follow- ers either become more cheerful, both subjectively and as consistent examples to those around them, or with more or less success simulated a modification of temperament in that respect, which nearly amounts in practice to the same thing. She taught charity in judging the deeds and motives of another," etc., etc.

This attitude of tolerance does more than gratify the followers of Mrs. Eddy, which we take it it does. It reflects the highest credit upon the American people, who are brave enough and fair enough to acknowledge an achievement without small jealousy. The more this spirit is encouraged the nearer shall we get to the real brotherhood of man and church unity.

Los Angeles Express, CA

Not merely one of the world's great women — one of the world's greatest personages passed away when Mary Baker Eddy died in Boston Saturday night. She must be adjudged great if measured only by the extent of the influence she exerted over the minds and lives of men and women over all the earth. That influence was world-wide and strongly potent in its workings, guiding and controlling the views of hundreds upon hundreds of thousands of exceptionally intelligent disciples. Whether her long career be regarded with reverent consideration or in hostile criticism, friend and foe must unite in the judgment that places among the group of the world's great, this woman, whose body now lies dead but whose spirit still strongly lives.

The change that men call death came softly and painlessly after four score years and ten of life devoted to the search for truth. Her search ended where all life begins — in God. Death found her work complete, her mission ended, her service fulfilled. The way she pioneered, the path she found, now runs broad and smooth to the feet of all who believingly follow. She made God easy of approach to hosts of men and women who, losing faith, else had not known Him. She gave vitality to belief, direction to aimless purpose, ideality to life, new sanctity to truth, supremacy to Mind, healing to the body, and did her part in bruising the serpent's head. It was a great creative work that Mary Baker Eddy achieved in an age when faith had begun to depart and belief to darken.

It is too early to measure the scope of her achievement. Although for years she has lived in retirement, perspective still is lacking. It is not in this generation or the next that it will be possible in the judgment of men to assign her to her rightful place. The work she did endures and will endure. Her teachings survive. Death has no power over truth. The church she founded, losing a founder, yet has lost but a member. It remains unhurt, the embodiment of principles, not a creation dependent for vitality upon an individual. While it continues faithful to Truth, and combative of error, a medium whereby increasingly is established the unity between life and God, it cannot die.

❊

Pasadena Daily News, CA

Whatever the partisan conviction of the average American churchman as to the permanent quality and present ethical and spiritual value of the religious faith of which Mrs. Eddy, the author of the text-book on Christian Science, was the acknowledged Leader, thinking people will at least pause to accord her that measure of justice and respect which her remarkable life, drawn out to the limit of almost ninety years, commands. Even in her old age she has been the object of the enmity of those who perhaps slightly understood her work and her real part in the realignment of the religious thought of the world.

Mrs. Eddy's remarkable book, it must be admitted by friends and critics alike, has resulted in one of the most wonderful religious developments of our time. It cannot be denied that its teachings have carried relief to hundreds of thousands of hopeless sufferers, many of them having exhausted every other possible source of relief. Whatever may be thought of its interpretation of spiritual truth, whatever may be the judgment of the world at this time of its logic, the fact remains that to suffering humanity it has been a boon. No intelligent, fair-minded person, in the face of the overwhelming evidence of the value of this belief in bringing health, mental sunshine, and cheer, in expelling suffering, fear, worry, and hate, can question that it is one of the great, potent, and virile religions, however they may differ from its point of view. It professes to be a religion of love and unshrinking trust.

The more religion the world can get, under whatever name, that will strengthen faith and relieve suffering, dispel discouragement, fear, and hate, the better for humanity. It is perhaps the common consensus of opinion that in this direction Mrs. Eddy's life and work has contributed its full part. Abuse and persecution has not retarded the growth of Christian Science. Its hold on men and women of discrimination, intelligence, and character, has been the most conspicuous development of modern religious thought.

Cleveland Leader, OH

One of the most remarkable women of the age, or of any age, has ended her career in the death of the Founder of Christian Science. The most bitter hostility to Mrs. Eddy and the most complete rejection of her doctrines and her church organization cannot, if honest and intelligent, deny that she has been a far-reaching and vital force in the thought and life of her times. The religion which she founded and completely dominated has more or less colored and permeated very important phases of existence for a multitude of men and women who do not call themselves Christian Scientists and are not, in fact, connected with the Christian Science organization.

Her doctrines and her great influence upon tens of thousands of intelligent people, in this country and other lands, was a wholesome antidote to the extreme materialism which is one of the distinctive characteristics of the age. In so far as her teachings were credited and her conclusions were accepted, the ideal was exalted and the sensual and sensuous weakened. The spirit became more and material things less important. Nor can it be denied, by those who are well informed, that the result of the remarkable growth of Christian Science has been to give peace of mind and more wholesome conditions of life in every sense to many of Mrs. Eddy's followers.

San Francisco Examiner

It will be difficult to the layman in either the religious or medical worlds to properly estimate at its true value the life and career of Mary Baker Eddy. This much, however, the unprejudiced must admit: She was a woman with a mentality strong enough to hold her own against as bitter a tide of hostile criticism as ever threatened to overwhelm any leader of a new thought. In spite of this hostility Mrs. Eddy established, here in the United States, a cult which is to-day an important factor in the religious and social life of the nation. The Christian Science church is a recognized moral, religious, and medical force. Its edifices are reared in nearly a thousand cities and towns. Its membership is large. Its growth has been rapid. Its influence reaches into every quarter of the civilized globe.

A woman who could in the short span of a generation — she did not found the church of which she was the Leader until 1879 — build so great an edifice upon so firm a foundation was more than an ordinary woman. She was a great woman. How great the future alone can determine, for the true greatness of a leader of a new thought can only be measured through the perspective of years.

Philadelphia Press

There have been various founders of faiths, in all ages, who showed that the appeal they made to an absolute unquestioned, undoubting trust and belief in the spiritual and in its immediate revelation to and knowledge by every human being who accepts and seeks it, meets a need in human nature. Whether this belief be logical and capable of proof or not, it exists; it has been preached by some conspicuous leader in almost every Christian century, and it has always had some acceptance and has often founded a new sect, communion, or church.

In no other instance in this country has this acceptance been so widely diffused, shared by so many or accompanied by such readiness to flock to a new church and to follow a new leader, as in the case of the Church of Christ, Scientist. No one in our day and few in any day have ever succeeded in this particular task as has Mrs. Eddy. She leaves great churches, great congregations, and tens of thousands who feel that their lives, their souls, and their bodies have been transformed by her teaching. Her influence has been great outside of her own following, and she has sensibly influenced the preaching and the teaching of many churches and the lives and thought of many who did not for an instant accept either her utterances or her claims.

Sandusky Register, OH

The death of Mrs. Mary Baker Eddy removes from the living one of the most remarkable women of the centuries. However people may differ about the doctrines she taught, however diverse human opinion may be as to her claims and her writings, whatever may be the final judgment of an intelligent Christian world concerning Christian Science, all must admit that she was a transcendent character. No other woman in modern times has ever reached anything like Mrs. Eddy's heights in leadership, in organization, and in enduring fame.

The church Mrs. Eddy founded but a few years ago already has a membership in this country of probably one hundred thousand, made up not of ignorant, credulous people, not of those who are easily duped, who are moved by prejudice and passion, but more largely than the average denominational church, of thoughtful people, educated people, intelligent and cultured people, drawn largely from the leading Protestant Christian churches throughout the world, a unique religious body unlike any other in history and yet holding to certain fundamental truths which people of all religious beliefs admit, a religious body having some of the finest edifices erected in modern times. Mrs. Eddy did not live in vain. The world has been made and will still be made the better for her having lived, and she has left an impress world-wide that will go down the centuries yet unborn.

Providence News, RI

Mrs. Eddy has been the subject of much comment, but that she was a great leader of men and women is proven by the many thousands of adherents that she secured in the most cultured sections of this country. The handsome church structures that the Christian Scientists have erected in Boston and this city indicate at least that they have a firm confidence in the continuance of their organization. Nothing is easier than to find fault with those who advocate changes of such a radical nature as did Mrs. Eddy, and yet the fact remains that, no matter what doubters may assert, many have found bodily health and more mental calm by reason of the attention given to the courses she advocated.

Mrs. Eddy had stanch friends and many earnest workers in her cause. She undoubtedly did much good, and whether one agrees with either the religious views she advanced or her belief in the all-powerful control of matter by mind, she alleviated much real distress and gave to men and women, many of them of undoubted sincerity, a new faith at least in themselves. Her long life, therefore, was a most useful one, and she will long be remembered as one of the remarkable personages of the last years of the connecting extremes of two progressive centuries.

Union, Sacramento, CA

In the death of Mrs. Eddy the world loses a woman who has been a very important influence in the uplifting of humanity. She has, during her lifetime, converted millions to her doctrines, and all over the country the effects of her teachings are visible.

In Mrs. Eddy the United States has lost one of its most valuable citizens and the world one of its most philanthropic and broad-minded women. The recent death of Tolstoi suggests a comparison between the two, for both were engaged in trying to elevate humanity, but while the Russian was always pessimistic and saw only the somber side of things, this good woman saw only the bright side and sought to accomplish her mission not with tears, but with smiles; not by sad prophecies for the future, but by giving to the world brighter and better hopes and truer ideas of happiness, both on this side of the grave and on the other.

Joplin Daily Globe, MO

Mrs. Eddy's death is the world event of a day because her life is a world event of the age. The verdict as to her place in literature, or philosophy, or theology, or medicine is unimportant. The verdict as to her place in the life-story of the world is stupendous; it "passeth all understanding." Now that she has gone the world will speculate upon the effect of her departure and will reconsider and gently qualify many of the harsh, unfair sentences it passed upon her. The profound scholarship, for illustration, that had penetrated the depths of the labyrinth of human knowledge may be accorded belated recognition. Men of letters may apprehend it to be their duty to read the book which in the artistry of its proportion, the felicity of its expression, the puissance of its logic, its rare grammatical purity, the splendor of its visions, and the sweetness of its message is, in simple truth, a book of books.

And as men of letters may do honor to her scholarship, so philosophy may lay aside its pride and its intolerance and pay homage to a service that retrieved contentment from the world's lost arts. So, too, may theology, grim and resentful, address in a spirit of fellowship, one other of "the wondrous names of God." And who shall say but medicine, grappling resolutely but hopelessly with its adversary, may ultimately accept this school of healing as an ally?

As a Leader, a teacher, and evangel that sought strange, independent channels for her energies, Mrs. Eddy is held in reverence and affectionate esteem by the army of a million recruited from all the ranks of life. And in the assurance she has brought to doubt, the hope with which she has routed despair, the strength that has been given to weakness, the courage that has supplanted cowardice, the health that has banished wretchedness, the glory of the everlasting day into which she has marshaled the wanderers in night's terror — thus, in the grandeur and the permanence and the mercy of her works, she stands justified. And by these tokens and imperishable signs the voice of a million reiterates, "There is no death."

Salt Lake Tribune

At a great age, Mrs. Eddy, the Founder and Leader of the Christian Science church, has passed away. She was a woman of very high ability along the lines which she chose or was led in her life-work. To formulate a system of belief, organize a church which spread with such strength and rapidity as the Christian Science church has done, and to retain the love, veneration, and devotion of such multitudes of her fellow-beings as Mrs. Eddy has done, shows the possession by her of qualities as remarkable as they were vital. It is idle to decry her or her work, in view of her resplendent success; to speak of a monument for her is but to ask for gilding to the fine gold of achievement for her work, and the church she founded will be her ever-present and most splendid memorial for all time. That work is a marvel, amazing to whoever will consider it candidly for what it is, and in its inception and growth. It is now one of the mighty factors in American life, and is still pushing on.

World-Herald, Omaha, NE

In some respects, at least, Mrs. Eddy seems, from the perspective of to-day, one of the world's great women. It is possible that she will some day be generally accepted as the world's greatest woman. She was the "Discoverer" of a religion and the Founder of a church. It is a religion that seems to make a universal appeal, in that it is accepted by men and women of all races, creeds, and conditions, and so it is a church that gives promise of enduring permanence. Philosophically it rests on the doctrine of pure idealism, morally on the gospel of love. A religion resting on such foundations, and satisfying, as it has from its inception, some of the purest souls and clearest minds of the present civilization, should travel far through the generations.

There can be general agreement as to the rare qualities of heart and mind and personality of Mrs. Eddy, the Founder of Christian Science. Like Tolstoi, she is one of the unique figures of universal history.

Evening Index, San Bernardino, CA

In the passing of Mary Baker Eddy there was removed from earthly existence the most beloved woman in history. The good citizenship will applaud the efforts of any one who helps humanity to a more correct life, no matter through what channel of religion. Therefore it would seem but the insincere who would fail to say aught but good of this noble woman. She faced the world, with its harsh criticism and ridicule, alone, with only her God as a protection. For years she stood with her faith unshaken by that which would have quailed the stoutest heart. First dozens, then hundreds, then thousands, then tens of thousands were appealed to by her religion and found relief from many worries of life, until to-day Christian Science reaches around the world and to its farthest corners.

In the beginning Mrs. Eddy said steadfastly, "God is my life;" her last earthly message was "God is my life."

Columbus News, OH

It must be admitted that Mrs. Eddy herself and her doctrinal school are among the powerful uplifting forces of this age. Even if its possible accomplishments have been exaggerated, as its antagonists contend, it cannot be denied that Christian Science has made mankind happier, healthier, and better. Judged by results, the life and teachings of this remarkable woman were rich in helpfulness to mankind.

Los Angeles Record, CA

In the passing of Mrs. Mary Baker Eddy, Founder and Leader of the Church of Christ, Scientist, this world has lost one of the most wonderful women it has ever known. Over two score years ago she discovered what she believed was the real religion taught in the Bible. Her ideas were ridiculed and attacked on every side. But she was not disheartened. She met all attacks, all opposition, calmly, bravely, as one who had the true courage of her convictions, and persevered. Little by little others came to believe as she did, and to-day the Christian Science movement has spread all over the world and has millions of faithful adherents, who daily thank God for His goodness, and give expression of their gratitude to Mrs. Eddy for her work in opening the door of this religion to them.

Although there are millions who believe in Christian Science, there are more millions who do not, but even the most bitter enemies must admit that Christian Science has done much to relieve suffering, and has brought health, happiness, and peace to hundreds of thousands who were ill, physically, morally, spiritually. Mrs. Eddy was a brilliant woman, a brave woman, and the world has been made better by her presence. Could she speak to-day, in the flesh, it seems as if she might fittingly say, as did Paul: "I have fought a good fight, I have finished my course, I have kept the faith: Henceforth there is laid up for me a crown of righteousness, which the Lord, the righteous judge, shall give me at that day; and not to me only, but unto all them also that love his appearing."

Kansas City Journal, MO

We of the present moment, lacking the gifts of prophecy or even of perspective, must estimate the life, character, and achievements of this Founder of a new religious and philosophic school on a basis of personal observation. To be just we must take rightful account of the wonderful influence of the Christian Science faith in our modern life. From ocean to ocean in this country stand the fashioned monuments to this movement, and engraven on each temple of Christian Science worship is the name of Mary Baker Eddy. Thousands of intelligent and serious-minded men and women have accepted her as their spiritual Leader. Her theories have brought solace to many a discouraged soul, and peace reigns in thousands of families where before was doubt, unhappiness, and dread. This much we know.

Thoughtful men and women, unblinded by prejudice, must pay a tribute of respect and admiration for this earnest and forceful character who made such an imprint upon modern thought.

Rutherford Republican, NJ

In the death of Mary Baker Eddy the world has lost a wonderful woman, one whose life's work will go down in church history as the equal of the Wesleys, Calvin, Luther, and others of like prominence in the promulgation and foundation of theological teachings and ethics. As in the case with these others, thousands of men and women the world over bless the memory of Mrs. Eddy for the countless benefits brought into their lives by her teachings. It makes little difference by what name it is called, any creed or ethical doctrine which makes the ordinary human being more content and happy in this life, more worthy to live it, and inspired with a confidence and hope of that which is beyond, is a precious blessing to mankind, and one whose benefits cannot be calculated by human measure. Such a blessing the deceased head of the Christian Science church has conferred upon innumerable human beings, and with a confidence and gratefulness born of personal experience and benefits, these will hold her and her teachings in reverential memory forever and anon.

The Iron Era, Dover, NJ

Mrs. Eddy's life-work has been crowned with wonderful success, criticized, perhaps, by those understanding it little or worse than not at all, but nevertheless rapidly gaining numerically and in influence as a faith. On all sides may be seen living and enthusiastic examples of the cures worked by this belief, and whether or not prejudice or belief or profession shall cause some to sneer at and decry the real cause of these healings, all mankind must admit that if the practice of the teachings of one woman shall have done so much for humanity, it was good for that woman to have lived among us.

New Era, South Bend, IN

Judged by her achievements, Mrs. Mary Baker Eddy was one of the extraordinary figures of the nineteenth century. Putting aside all claims for the wonderful healing ascribed to the following of her teaching, one great practical good is apparent from her efforts, and that is the stimulation they have given to the reading and careful studying of the Scriptures by thousands of her followers, who by their optimistic views of life make their earthly journey one of hope and confidence born of a great love toward their Maker. To them the golden rule is the cardinal doctrine of conduct in their relations with their fellow-beings, and possessing, as they do, an abiding faith in their destiny, they face the world with a serenity of mind that adds greatly to the joys of life.

At this time it is proper to recognize the dimensions of her practical achievements and the claims which her remarkable personality and her creed have upon the world's attention and regard.

✗➒

Los Angeles Herald, CA

The history of womankind has no parallel to the career of Mary Baker Eddy and its effects on the lives of others, and the woman who passed away at her home in Brookline, Massachusetts, on Saturday night can be said to have directly influenced more persons than any other of her sex either in ancient or modern times. Considered either as a spiritual leader or as to her personality in its more human aspects, Mrs. Eddy was a most wonderful woman.

Considered apart from her religious position this can be

said of Mrs. Eddy: The world owes her gratitude for show-
ing how closely sobriety and temperance in act and
thought (and the converse) may affect body and spirit alike.
If the result of her efforts had only caused the multiplied
thousands of her adherents to live more orderly lives and
be examples to a headlong age, she would not have lived in
vain.

Brunswick Record, ME

The death of Mrs. Eddy at the age of ninety years brings to
public attention the wonderful work she has accomplished.
No one can doubt that she was a woman of rare power and
intellect. Thousands have become her followers, learned
the lessons which she has taught, and produced the results
she has desired in the upbuilding of the Christian Science
church. Aside from her teachings and the Christian Science doctrines, it is only fair to say that in so far as she has
brought peace, happiness, and health to mankind she
should be respected and honored.

Boston Journal

There is no little significance in the fact that the Founder
of Christian Science will be taken to Mount Auburn, her

last resting-place, to-day with simple ceremony. It is even more significant that in the messages received by the church authorities from all parts of the world there is no note of sadness or of disturbance regarding the future. If for nothing else, then for the simplicity and the serenity which she inculcated by precept and practice, Mrs. Eddy has deserved the tributes that since Sunday have been appearing here and abroad. In an age which has been making special reports on neurasthenia, it is remarkable, if not positively providential, that through the agency of a woman, the world should have received partial relief by the exercise of a faith that was not permitted to backslide. There is great good in most beliefs. In this particular case that good was realized by steadfast practice of a gospel. It is a lesson which even those who run may read.

Kansas City Star

Mrs. Mary Baker Eddy was one of the remarkable personages of the long period of time her life inclosed. She was the moving spirit in and the chief exemplar of a religious and spiritual phenomenon affecting in some degree nearly the whole of the civilized world. The Founder of the Christian Science church developed a way of life and a spiritual creed by which many thousands of persons have found serenity of mind and a correlative physical well-being. In her own mind and body she exemplified the value of her teachings. Her long life closed amid the spiritual veneration and love of hundreds of thousands of associated religionists and the kindly esteem of almost the whole world.

Post-Dispatch, St. Louis, MO

There is convincing evidence of the potent and lasting influence of Mrs. Eddy's work. It is difficult at this time to measure its effect. It has profoundly influenced religious thought and has modified medical science and practice. Mrs. Eddy's views on Mind as the only power and reality, and her method of applying the Christian ideal as a practical working force to the problems of daily life, have been accepted as revelations of truth by hosts of people. Her extraordinary power and influence are recognized by her bitterest opponents. She has a unique place among religious leaders and thinkers.

Springfield Republican, MO

Mrs. Eddy had done very much for the world, too. That must be admitted regardless of what one's position may be regarding her teachings. She lived a beautiful life, she taught other to live as cleanly. She taught hope and trust and happiness and goodness. She caused a great deal of all those principles to become the guiding influence in the daily living of people who believed in her, — an influence which has come to touch a very great portion of the earth.

Houston Chronicle, TX

The death of Mrs. Eddy is regretted throughout the United States. The Founder of Christian Science was a remarkable woman. Whatever those opposed to her teachings may think of Christian Science and the great Christian Science Leader, there is no doubt that she brought religious faith to many previously without it and her general influence on the world was good.

Daily Argus-Leader, Sioux Falls, SD

The great influence which Mrs. Eddy exerted on the religious thought of her day will not be lost with her passing away. Her work will go on, and undoubtedly history will accord her a place with the great religious leaders of the Christian era.

Twentieth Century Magazine

Mrs. Mary Baker Eddy, the Founder of Christian Science, passed into the broader life on December 3, in her ninetieth year. The story of her life forms one of the most remarkable records among the histories of the religious leaders of the ages, and she was unquestionably the greatest religious leader that has arisen in the new world. To those who knew her personally and intimately she was the incarnation of love and kindliness of spirit, though resolute and brave in uncovering and opposing error. Seldom in the history of civilization has a great spiritual leader lived to see so rich fruition follow the giving of the message.

From infancy, her health was frail. Many of her early years were years of constant suffering and pronounced invalidism, and after seeming restoration to health came an accident that brought her to the gates of death. This was more than fifty years ago. When hope from human sources had been abandoned, she experienced an interior illumination or a realization of the power of God to heal. Since then, for over half a century, she wrought indefatigably, giving to the world the message she believed to have come from the All-Father as a new illumination, revealing anew the Christ-truth that made the early and uncorrupted church invincible.

For more than half a century, the most powerful opposition and antagonisms beat around her. For years and decades she was the target for ridicule, abuse, slander, and calumny. Conventional religion and organized medicine vied with each other in attacking her theory, ridiculing her position and impugning her motives. Foes arose within her own household, and to the fierce opposition that has almost always beaten with tempestlike force around the head of a great religious or spiritual leader, was added the opposition of organized medicine, only second to dogmatic theology in its intolerance for new theories or philosophical concepts that antagonize old ideas. The persistent, tireless, and many-sided opposition would have crushed any one not sustained by an invincible living faith. In an hour when the creeping paralysis of materialism was taking hold of conventional Christianity, making it increasingly blind to the spirit and correspondingly concerned with the exterior manifestation, Mrs. Eddy gave forth her message, which has transformed hundreds of thousands of lives.

One does not have to be a Christian Scientist to recognize the wonderful work it has already wrought. If it had done nothing more than heal tens of thousands of hopeless invalids, thousands of whom were resting under the death sentence from conventional medical scholasticism, it would have done much. If it had done nothing more than transform and ennoble with a vital faith hundreds of thousands of lives to which God and religion had come to mean nothing, it would have been one of the greatest positive upward-impelling forces of the age. That this message should appeal in a compelling way to a million or more intelligent men and women in the most searching and critical age and among the most mentally acute peoples of earth, is one of the most significant historic facts of the present.

Argus-Leader, Sioux Falls, SD

There are few women of this age whose names are more familiar in the average home than that of Mrs. Mary Baker Eddy. There are few who have been the object of such extremes in the expressed opinion of the public as has this able woman, who in middle life, after a long period of seclusion, emerged with a wonderful system of religion, that within a few years has extended its influence to the uttermost parts of the earth.

Her faith has weathered the taunts and the gibes and the persecution of the majority, and has brought peace and comfort and usefulness to an ever-increasing minority of her fellow-beings. We who know the least of the woman and her work have perhaps been their severest critics. It has been easy to follow up the recital of cures effected by Christian Science with the remark that it was a wonderful thing, and it was accomplishing a great work among people who were ailing only in imagination. We have delighted in recounting cases where Christian Science patients have died for want of medical assistance. Perhaps they have; but in order to have been just, we should have struck a balance with the fatalities due to too much surgical and medical experiment.

Leaving the subject of physical healing to the discussion of the learned and wise, let us simply look into the faces of the pupils of Mary Baker Eddy. There we read the message of "On earth peace, good will to men," and bask in a momentary reflection of the radiant joy that seems to illumine the lives of all her followers. The strained, hurried, worried, hunted look characteristic of our modern existence has been smoothed away as completely as the hand of death erases all trace of physical suffering on the faces of our dear ones, filling us with awe at its mystery and its sublimity. As light hearts and happy faces are as infectious as their too numerous antipodes, the influence of Mrs. Eddy's teachings reaches far out beyond the pale of her following and, regardless of religious or scientific belief, sends shafts of warm light into thousands of shadowed lives.

Surely she has not lived and wrought in vain! We may neither understand nor accept for ourselves her teachings, but in recognition of her efforts and of her success, as we must see it, in humanity's cause, we tenderly lay a wreath of laurels on her bier and carve her name on the tablets of memory among those of many other brave women of this century, who have blazed the way through dark forests of public disapproval and tangled thickets of persecution into the clear light of Truth as seen by them.

Short Hills Item, NJ

Mrs. Eddy's greatness came from rediscovering and restoring the method of Christ's healing. Her book, *Science and Health with Key to the Scriptures,* contains the rule by which to find one's relation to God and the resultant freedom from every evil that flesh is heir to. It is a book that must be studied to be understood, and hundreds of thousands to-day claim that it has introduced them to better morals, firm health, and a satisfying religion of the "I know" quality. To understand is to know. Understanding changes blind faith to realization — to knowing. Wisdom, godliness, and health may be attained by the practice of the teachings of Science and health in connection with the Scriptures, and all, if they will, may demonstrate it. This happy consummation can be brought about not by retaining in consciousness old-time cherished but erroneous theories and beliefs, but by dismissing them, and putting in their place Mrs. Eddy's demonstrable truth as taught in the Bible and in her writings. This is not mere assertion, — it is fact — fact that may be stubborn, and yet gloriously so. Multitudes are proclaiming most solemnly and happily these facts. These multitudes are composed of intelligent, progressive persons in search of ultimate truth, — who do not want unsubstantiated theories, but who do want religious facts scientifically demonstrated in the Christ-way right in their own consciousness and experience. The remedy for all sin and error and all discord and all disease, as taught by Mrs. Eddy, is Truth, and Jesus said, "Ye shall know the truth, and the truth shall make you free."

We thank Mrs. Eddy because she demands as did her Master the perfect life, and because she shows us how it can be accomplished. We thank her for reinstating the Christ-religion and proving it such by practical demonstration. We thank her for a religion that knows one God only. We thank her for founding and establishing a church scientifically Christian. We thank her for her "Key" that opens the spiritual Bible. We thank her for steadfastly continuing her studies in humanity's behalf under inhuman persecution; for her genuinely Christian life, without which it would have been impossible for her to become great in humanity's service.

The pages of the world's history fail to reveal a greater woman either in one or in many accomplishments. Mrs. Eddy was without a superior among her sex for spiritual insight, organization, and leadership, and in capacity for indefatigable labor. Her writings, including hymns and poems, are permanent literature, ever refreshing, ever sought, growing more and more appreciated. Rejoicingly affirming "God is my life," she entered upon her higher consciousness, beautifully, triumphantly.

Beacon, Cannon Falls, MN

Those things that we call character in the individual are expressed in the sum total of the life-work; and the ability to work in this sense is also measured by the ability of the individual to lose himself in his work. Work to be of lasting value must be a share of the general work to be done; the lasting good one does, a part of the general good. History shows this to be the one true measure of greatness, and since Mrs. Eddy's work, both as a system of healing and as a religious philosophy, long since passed the experimental point and has become an institution, so Mrs. Eddy's place in the history of her country and of all countries, of the religion of her time and of all times, is defined and certain.

Mrs. Eddy was a great soul rather than a great intellect;

though as a philosophical thinker and writer she looms large, it was in the realm where the philosophical and the spiritual commingle, in the philosophy of the spiritual, that she specially shone and where she was specially strong and effective. And this expresses, too, the most striking feature of Mrs. Eddy's work; it was effective, — widely and amazingly effective. Though her thought, as expressed in *Science and Health* and her other writings, was often involved — as is often unavoidable in dealing with subjects that do not accommodate themselves to the foot-rule system of elucidation — her language was always most simple and even her most earnest controversial style was kindly. Nothing was ever more clearly demonstrated in the life-work of an individual than was the spirituality, the kindly nature and the human understanding of Mrs. Eddy demonstrated in her work. This, too, was one of the obvious causes of her effectiveness as a leader and teacher. No one at all familiar through Christian Science publications with the tone of the many letters addressed to her from Christian Scientists from all parts of the world where civilization has gained a foothold, could doubt that Mrs. Eddy was deeply beloved by a great multitude of people, whom she had won to her by the wisdom, the sincerity, the sympathy, the forbearance and what might we think be called the keen spirituality evident in her written work. That Mrs. Eddy's life, energies, and talents were devoted to the general good is evident, not only in the million or more who are identified with the Christian Science church, but in the millions more who through contact with the movement have been restored to health, through its system of healing, and strengthened, blessed, and comforted by its spiritual philosophy.

Piqua Leader-Dispatch, OH

Founder of the Christian Science cult, it cannot be denied that her life, her work, her faith have done untold good, and doubtless it will be admitted that in the church she founded, fostered, and furthered, her good works shall go on. Thus, even in that aspect it cannot be said that Mary Baker Eddy is dead. Death nowadays has come to mean so little to the broadened mind of advancing civilization that, when a great mind and a pure spirit pass beyond the ken of our limited vision or expression, we have begun to dimly realize that death could mean no cessation of usefulness.

Thus with Mrs. Eddy. Agree with or admire her as we may; disagree with or scoff at her as we will, she leaves behind a feeling of power, of purpose, of accomplishment, and of a faith so strong that we are forced to admit that death is but a fleeting breath that has passed over the flickering light of human life, or a shadow that has passed between our vision and the object of our comprehension. The great souls are still here, and, but that our eyes are dimmed, our vision limited, we should still be in touch and communication with them.

That she died does not in any way detract from the seriousness of the teachings of Christian Science. Other great Christian disciples have died, but their religion goes on, and so may the teachings of Mary Baker Eddy. Much more than the peace of mind of the Christian Scientists — which even the greatest enemies of the cult confess exists among her followers — must lie in this belief. The church has grown too large and has too many eminent thinkers in its congregations for any general acceptance that the belief merely eases the worries of life. However, if it did nothing more, and is accepted for only this, what a great boon to mankind has been this woman, whose life, lived in our time, may a hundred years hence seem as marvelous as that of some of the other great teachers that made the worship in the Christian religion one of the great institutions of civilization.

Jewish Review and Observer, Cleveland, OH

The death of Mary Baker Eddy, the Founder of Christian Science, removes from the world a great leader of superior ability, and while we do not agree with her in her religious doctrines, we must acknowledge that she was one of the greatest women of modern times, and that it was largely due to her remarkable powers as a leader that Christian Science has secured the large number of followers. Although Mrs. Eddy is dead, Christian Science will live.

Aroostook Pioneer, Houlton, ME

In the death of the founder of Christian Science, America has lost another of its greatest women. However much we may have disagreed with her or have criticized her utterances, we can but admit her greatness and the remarkable power she had of leading. She founded a religious sect that has shaken the foundations of every evangelical church in the country. Her life has added one more proof that humanity longs for a belief in the spiritual, for trust in a higher power, and for visual evidence of its agency. Mrs. Eddy's religion appealed to the sick, the afflicted, and the hypochondriac, where others appealed to the outcast and the forsaken. She won largely, and the force of her character will be felt in her church for all time. Regardless of the merits or demerits of Christian Science, it has become an unmistakable influence of the century. Mrs. Eddy built a church which has drawn to it persons of culture, education, and property, and we have no doubt that it will go on, accepting what we call the death of its Leader as only one more demonstration of her greatness.

Saratogian, Saratoga Springs, NY

The public may well heed the very useful and desirable lesson emphasized at the recent funeral of Mrs. Eddy, Founder and Leader of the Christian Science church — that of simplicity and lack of show and ostentation at such ceremonies. Mrs. Eddy was the Leader of a following of many hundreds of thousands of persons. To her as the Founder of their religious belief they naturally gave great love and veneration. Naturally they would desire to show at her death some measure of their grief and sentiment. The opportunity was presented for much of display and ceremony and fulsome tribute. But it was not utilized. On the contrary, there was no parading of grief, no array of eulogy disbursers, no costly ostentation, and little of the outward show of paraded grief and funeral trappings.

All of which was eminently sensible and proper. The average funeral eulogy is a farce. The usual display at such a time is grossly out of place. A burden of debt is habitually incurred that is wrong in every sense and often a great hardship to those who are directly concerned in meeting it.

Such display and expense assuage in no way the sorrow of mourners or the peace of the departed. If Christian Science teaches the more sensible way, it is doing a great service to humanity.

Boston Courier, MA

Whatever may be the prevailing opinion as to the tenets of her faith and its lasting benefit to the great cause of religion, none can deny that Mrs. Eddy was a remarkable personality, one of the great characters which stand out in bold relief in the history of the nineteenth century in spiritual affairs. Long after many who have won renown in literature, in art, in social and political advancement shall be forgotten with the passing years, her name will live as the Founder of a great religious cult which has taken firm hold of the souls and consciences of millions of the human race and has extended to the farthest limits of civilization. To her genius, her inspiration, her mental and spiritual powers alone the world owes the great religious movement of Christian Science. From humble origin it has risen in the short space of thirty years to include in its devotees some of the most intellectual and wealthiest among the English-speaking people. Her leadership was accepted without qualification or rivalry, and most graciously she has exercised the control and spiritual direction so freely accorded to her. She has brought to herself the power of concentration and a devotion which alone would have marked her as a character of eminence.

The record of Christian Science has been phenomenal. What a rise and progress it has had! No other faith in the world's history, as far as human annals go, has risen and extended so rapidly, so quietly, so persistently. The cause projected by her, nourished patiently and almost despondingly amid the misgivings of friends and reproaches of enemies, triumphed in the moment of despair. It was an individual triumph. It showed the implicit confidence in the germs of truth at the base of her belief, and the stability of her faith. The fact that the cause has extended so far, that it has drawn so many adherents, that her precepts and sayings are regarded as an inspiration to her followers, is an acknowledgment of her great individuality.

Evening Tribune, Des Moines, IA

In the death of Mrs. Eddy the United States loses one of the most remarkable women of her time. Whatever may be thought of the faith she founded, the fact that she founded a faith, intelligent people by hundreds of thousands profess in these intellectual days of scientific caution, marks her a prodigy. Moreover, her faith, instead of being gross or materialistic, has been idealistic to a degree, so much so that to the unbeliever it has seemed fanciful, a remarkable faith to gain adherents for in a practical age, when belief is confined very largely to things seen.

Billings Journal, Billings, MT

With the passing of the acknowledged Founder and Leader of the Christian Science church organization, there departed from this life one of the most remarkable women the world has ever known. It is not necessary to be a believer in the religious tenets she propounded to realize this fact, nor does appreciation of her stupendous labors depend in any manner upon acceptance of their verity. Call her inspiration by whatever term you choose, it is still undeniably true that her teachings were accepted without question by a very large number of unusually intelligent men and women upon whose lives was exerted as powerful an influence for good — both material and spiritual — as has ever been recorded in the history of civilization.

Apart from and independent of any doctrinal feature of the Church of Christ, Scientist — a discussion of which would not be proper in a secular newspaper — there towers the supreme personality of its Founder. Forceful, and dominating by the power of spiritual strength, she won and held a loyalty seldom accorded the pioneer in a religious movement. The persistence of her thought was a mighty force that convinced where doubt existed and broke down the barriers erected by mental opposition to a degree that has been the marvel of her age.

Coupled with a positive genius for organization, there was a depth of sincerity and a profound earnestness which illumined the written word as much as the spoken sentence and brought heart and mind of her followers captive to the central precept she sought to inculcate, and she believed no more implicitly than did they in the essential quality of its divine origin. Such power to sway others is seldom met with in all the records of all times, and its effect cannot be other than vital upon the life and destiny of the human race, in the history of which few personalities have been more impressive than that of the aged woman from whose mortal frame the masterful spirit has finally departed.

Harlem Local, New York City

Whatever difference of views may be entertained by those who are not connected with that great and growing religious organization as to its merits and benefits to mankind, there can be no doubt as to the sincerity of the remarkable woman who originated and promulgated the principles and doctrines of that faith. The movement which Mrs. Eddy began less than forty years ago has increased in its influence and power to an extent that has surprised even her followers, notwithstanding the virulent assaults that have been made upon it, and within the past few years many of the most cultured and eminent men and women in this country have become closely identified with the Christian Science church. The fundamental basis of the newfound faith is that God is omnipotent and omnipresent good, and where He exists evil cannot prevail; that man was created in His image and likeness, and that Jesus Christ was the perfect and immaculate incarnation of His character.

Mrs. Eddy announced, as she doubtless believed, that "divine Love always has met and always will meet every human need" (*Science and Health,* p. 494), and that the man who loves God will also love his fellow-men under all circumstances and conditions. Christian Scientists believe that if their faith were universally accepted there would be no need of battleships, armories, fortifications, hospitals, almshouses, prisons, police, nor criminal courts, and that Mr. Carnegie's admirable system to encourage temperance would be entirely useless and unnecessary; all of which is only another reawakening of the spirit of the teachings of the holy Scriptures.

Utica Press, NY

The death of Mrs. Mary Baker Eddy, the Leader of the Christian Science church, removes a remarkable woman, whose activities were continued till her ninetieth year. Whatever anybody may think about the doctrines she taught or the church she founded, it must be conceded by her severest critic that she was a woman of exceptional ability in several directions, and that her equal has been seldom seen.

It is a great achievement to have built up in practically three decades a church as large as that founded by the deceased. She wrote *Science and Health* in 1875, began preaching in 1878, and organized The First Church of Christ, Scientist, at Boston in 1879. Since then the growth has been phenomenal, till now there is scarcely a community of any size in the country where this denomination is not represented. One need not subscribe to it or agree with it to accord honest respect to those who do believe in it, for this is a free country in which everybody is entitled to absolute personal freedom in matters of this sort. Surely the Christian Scientists are good citizens, honorable and upright, and that is as far as the public has any concern. To Mrs. Eddy must be paid the tribute of exceptional ability as a leader and an executive, and those who have faith in her regard her with an affection that knew no bounds.

San Diego Herald, CA

The passing of Mrs. Eddy removes from the world's stage the most wonderful woman in all the world's history. As the Founder of a great religion, she lived to see her adherents swell to greater numbers than was ever known in the lifetime of one (except Mahomet) who preached a new doctrine. As mourning for departed friends was not favored by the great Leader, she will be missed more and mourned less than any prominent leader in the world. The people of this sect have enjoyed more practical and satisfactory benefits from their religion than have those of any religion ever promulgated.

Weatherford Democrat, TX

With the death of Mrs. Eddy, head of the Christian Science church, another rare and splendid character has passed away. Her faith was not our faith, though that is not to say she was wrong. In groping through the fogs and mist she may have come nearer to the truth than we. Anyway, it was her mission to do nothing but good, and the world is better because she lived. In the sweep of the centuries, there are few such souls that come to dwell on earth.

Mercury, San Jose, CA

Mrs. Eddy's death comes at a time when the church is not only vast numerically but potential financially. She carried it through the days of its childhood, on up to its present comparative maturity, and passed away idolized by thousands and with the knowledge that a monument is left to her memory such as has been the privilege of few women. It is inconceivable that Christian Science has been able to satisfy its thousands of devotees with a simple panacea for mental derangements. Had it not restored large numbers of bodies to normal health, it could never have had an indefinite lease of life and the ability to attract to its fold intellectual people of all races.

Mrs. Eddy was one of the most remarkable women of her day. In the face of bitter persecution and the almost unanimous opposition of society, she held fast to her faith until finally her sect became so formidable that her traducers either quit the conflict or joined her followers. Whether her Science is what it claims to be still remains a matter of opinion. But that those who believe in it have the same right to their faith as those who believe in other forms of worship there is no denying. In this country religion is left to a man's own choice. What is helpful to one may be destructive to another. It all depends on the view-point, and perhaps a little on the temperament.

Mrs. Eddy's Christian Science is here, and, we should say unhesitatingly, to stay. Like other religions it will have its defenders and its critics until the end. In the meantime, no just man or woman will withhold from Mrs. Eddy the meed of praise which her great accomplishment as one of the world's most brilliant executives and organizers deserves.

Goodwin's Weekly, Salt Lake City, UT

Mary Baker Eddy was a great woman. Foes as well as friends must admit that. She kindled a new light on earth. Some said it was a bale-fire, such as robbers build upon the seashore to lure passing ships upon the breakers; others that it was the real star of Bethlehem, signaling a closer walk between the children of men and the dwellers in the clear light in the realms where light had its birth. Thousands and millions believe her a new prophetess; millions have been comforted by her, thousands and tens of thousands who were afflicted have been comforted and healed by the ministrations she prescribed. It is not for one who does not comprehend her to judge of her, but it is only justice to say she wrought a marvelous work on earth; gave peace and serenity and health to tens and hundreds of thousands of homes. She was a priestess of a faith which was broad enough to encompass all the children of men; she was as self-contained as a second Hypatia, and one sovereign proof of her power was that when assailed she not only met the assaults with a superb serenity, but so impressed her followers that they, too, had nothing but pity for her assailants.

She lived here on earth twenty years beyond man's allotted time, then, unafraid, and with faculties undimmed, without a sigh, sank peacefully into her final sleep. The impression she leaves is perhaps the most profound that any mortal, putting on immortality, has left in this age.

Rochester Times, NY

The death of Mrs. Mary Baker Eddy marks the passing of a woman who is probably the most notable of this generation; certainly none other has had more widespread influence or is regarded with greater reverence by more people. The church or creed which she founded has spread to all parts of the world, has millions of followers, and among those followers are included some of the most intellectual and cultured persons of every community.

Personally, Mrs. Eddy was a woman of a most lovable character. Abuse of all sorts had been showered on her at different times in her career, but she bore it with a patience which ultimately disarmed many of her critics. She had been termed an impostor by many persons, but in recent years the world had come to take a fairer view of her. Whatever may be said of the tenets of the creed she taught, one thing is certain — no man or woman ever founded such a creed, which spread to all sections of the world and has made millions of converts, who was not absolutely sincere in her own belief in that creed or religion.

Evening Journal, Wilmington, DE

Mrs. Mary Baker Eddy, who passed away on Saturday night, may be regarded without exaggeration as the most remarkable woman of her times. Her hold upon her followers was indeed wonderful. In a day when all questions of a religious nature are subjected to the most critical tests, when some boast that the statements and influences of men of regular science have great weight and tend to demolish religious theories and principles of the past, Mrs.

Eddy founded a religious denomination which has grown and prospered in a very remarkable manner. Her adherents have been and are of a type of high intelligence.

One thing evident about the true Christian Scientists, which shows the powerful and beneficial influence that Mrs. Eddy has exerted in the world, is that they are firm in the faith, energetic and relentless in upholding it, and to all outward appearances in their lives are most happy. The religion founded by Mrs. Eddy has brought peace to many a distressed soul. After all, what higher benefit could it confer?

Morning American, Creston, IA

The death of Mrs. Eddy has removed from earth one of the greatest characters that the world has ever produced. This wonderful woman in the course of a few years has organized one of the greatest Christian organizations of the country. She was a leader of strong personality. She was an organizer of remarkable ability. She built up a church having as its leaders and expounders men of great minds and strong characters. Whether we agree with her doctrines or not there are thousands of men and women who will testify to the efficacy of curing by prayer, so that the Christian Science church is not merely a church of belief, but it is a militant church that brings to its believers physical as well as spiritual regeneration. We believe Mrs. Eddy had done a great work in the world for good.

Kansas City Journal, MO

Thousands of women who do not believe in Christian Science feel proud of Mrs. Eddy's achievements. Few men have wielded so great an influence over the minds and lives of so many people as this philosophic woman.

Springfield News, IL

Mrs. Mary Baker Eddy lived long enough to see the Science which she founded become one of the permanent and uplifting forces of Christendom. It is about thirty-five years ago that Mrs. Eddy published her now famous book, known as *Science and Health with Key to the Scriptures,* and it was four years later that the first Christian Science church was formed with seventeen members. To-day there are nearly a thousand chartered churches, nearly four thousand recognized practitioners, and a total church-membership of a million souls.

Something of an achievement to be accomplished in thirty-five years, and all within the lifetime of the Founder.

Eagle, Wichita, KS

Probably no other American woman by her own efforts ever performed such stupendous work. The vehemence of controversy which has been heaped upon her labors indicates the genius of the leadership which has overcome such vast opposition.

Mrs. Eddy rallied disciples around her until the followers of her teachings have spread over the world, numbering not thousands but hundreds of thousands. Even the layman of controversial bent who finds in Mrs. Eddy's work much that is intangible and to him meaningless, grants that he has tangible evidence of work for the good of mankind in the thousands of persons who credit to Mrs. Eddy's work their rescue from direful experiences.

St. Paul Dispatch, MN

There may be two opinions upon Christian Science; there can be but one opinion on Mary Baker Eddy. She was unquestionably one of the dominant influences of the age, one of the most remarkable of its women, perhaps the most remarkable, certainly the most efficient. And she so represents and permeates the cult known as "Christian Science" that to give her important rank is to give her teaching important meaning.

It must also be admitted that the sweeping influence of this "Science" could not have been had not the "Science" itself contained the truth and answered what was plainly a very large human need. It is entirely possible, notwithstanding the adverse criticism, the mirthful criticism, that Christian Science has within it truth, whether new or old, which shall withstand contemporary criticism and the neglect of time. If so, then the personal triumph of Mary Baker Eddy will be great and lasting.

Lincoln Daily Star, NE

One of the most remarkable women of this or any other age passed from the scene of worldly activity when Mary Baker Eddy went to sleep to wake no more to mortal consciousness. There may have been women whose personality stood out in more marked contrast with her kind, who were more spectacular, and made more noise in the everyday life of a somewhat noisy world; but for far-reaching and enduring effect upon mankind, the work of this woman who has just passed away at her home in Boston is unparalleled by that of any other woman of ancient or modern times.

Christian Science owes to Mary Baker Eddy the hold it has secured upon the devotional spirit of mankind, and every adherent of its church holds her in reverential memory. Her death will occasion world-wide regret and sorrow, although her span of life has been as long in years as her usefulness could survive. Her work will live after her indefinitely, possibly until the end of time. Her life has been a lesson of what her teachings can accomplish.

Among the great women of the world there has been none who has left so great an impress as has Mrs. Eddy.

Harper's Weekly

The tone of the newspaper comments on the death of Mrs. Eddy indicates a decided increase of respect in recent years both for her character and for her achievements. Nor is it a case of "*de mortuis nil nisi bonum,*" but a taking of one consideration with another, and giving a judgment of net approbation. Thus, to quote two of our more thoughtful and mentally exacting contemporaries, the *Sun* speaks of "the astonishing influence she exerted in thousands of homes for the amelioration of life and manners in some of the details of family and social intercourse," teaching cheerfulness of spirit and charity in judging deeds and motives. The *Springfield Republican* says her life was a marvel, and that having stumbled upon the truth that the influence of mind over body is really profound and far-reaching, the credit cannot be denied her of having forced, however extravagantly, the valuable qualities of this principle of therapeutics upon the world.

Certainly Mrs. Eddy, and the theories, and practical applications of them, with which she is so closely associated, have had a notable influence on certain phases of the thought of her time. She was a pioneer — one of the most extraordinary of whom there is a record — and there are few now who doubt that the body of facts and experience which has resulted from her pioneering is a valuable gain to knowledge.

Christian Advocate, Dallas, TX

After all, newspaper reports to the contrary notwithstanding, the late Mrs. Mary Baker Eddy, Founder and conservator of Christian Science, did leave considerable money to her son, his children, her adopted son, and several other beneficiaries. However, the bulk of her great fortune was bequeathed to the church founded by her genius and ability. Her fortune came to her largely through her book *Science and Health with Key to the Scriptures,* and numerous other writings. During her life she was liberal with her means, and in no sense can she be said to have been a woman of penurious nature. In various ways and to various humane institutions she opened her hand and scattered much of her annual income, and now in death it all goes largely to sustain the cause set upon foot by her life-work.

The Alaska Citizen, Fairbanks, AK

All over the world are homes which have been brightened by the doctrine taught by this truly great woman. Through her works a new religion has been established, and has taken root wherever Christianity is practised. While by no means universally accepted as all-embracing, even its opponents are compelled to admit that it achieves with thousands that uplift they have vainly sought through other teachings. And there is little doubt that this new religion is sufficiently well founded to insure of its enduring for all time. In the earlier period of the era of Christian Science, Mrs. Eddy found her task a heavy one; for, like the Saviour, she was reviled and discredited by the scoffers. It was then her Christian fortitude was evidenced to a marked degree, and her calm refusal to be goaded into reprisals undoubtedly won many thousands to her cause.

In the death of Mrs. Eddy the world has lost a teacher

whose doctrines have become, in two decades, more wide-spread, and have been adopted to a greater degree, than those of any man or woman who has lived in the past hundred years. That those teachings have been for the world's betterment will be most eagerly acknowledged by the many followers who to-day mourn her death.

✻

Syracuse Journal, NY

Mary Baker Eddy has done that in this world which will make her live and live. Her work is the greatest monument. She has given a calm to many lives which has surpassed that of many philosophies.

✻

Overland China Mail, Hong Kong

Confirmation was received on the ninth in Hong Kong, by private wire from Boston, of the death of Mrs. Eddy, Founder of Christian Science, which we announced on Monday. It was in 1875 that the first edition of *Science and Health* appeared, and Mrs. Eddy's followers now can be numbered by thousands in nearly every land. She was undoubtedly a wonderful woman, and one who won the unquestioning, whole-hearted support of those who believed in her teachings.

✝

Morning Star, Rockford, IL

Mary Baker Eddy was a remarkable woman, one of the greatest the world has ever known. The daughter of plain New England parents, who were deeply religious and who bequeathed their stern religious views to her, she became the founder of a sect which in this country is estimated to have a membership of a million. This great following was built up within little more than three decades. In its corner-stone was "heal the sick" and that millions were healed is not gainsaid. She founded her faith on the Bible, on the teachings of the "great healer."

She knew the Bible as few knew it, indeed to her its meanings and teachings were as sure and understandable as the alphabet. From cover to cover it contained no doubt and not a line bore a misgiving. It was inspired and stood for the betterment of mankind. It not only healed the mind but the body. It was a sheet anchor, and clinging to it meant physical and spiritual safety. These were her teachings, and whether we believe in them or not, we must admit that she did measureless good. That she was actuated by good purposes and sought the ennoblement of her fellows cannot be denied.

Mrs. Eddy taught that life is beautiful as it becomes pure. She taught there is no death as the pagan saw it, but that to pass from this death was to pass into the land of the forever. Though she has gone, Truth, as she understood it, will never perish.

><♣>

Arizona Sentinel, Yuma, AZ

Sunday there passed from the life of this world — not from its cares, for she had risen above them all — the greatest of all women — Mary Baker Eddy, the Founder of Christian Science. From the present day back to where disappear in the mists of tradition the initial mileposts of Aryan civilization, paralleling the achievement records of the world's super men, the pages of history are resplendent with the glory of earth's great women. Viewed from a broad perspective, however, they stand a sisterhood of similarity — all save one. Like her there was none.

Excepting her alone, the great women of history gained heritage to supremacy through lavish bestowals of nature in prodigal mood. Great beauty had they, or great wit, or overdominant will and mentality equal to masculinity. None of these had she. Not hers the magnificence of Sheba's queen, the splendor of Semiramis, the passion of Cleopatra, the militant spirit of Maria Theresa, the brutality of Catherine, the grace of Marie Antoinette or the wit of Madame de Staël. Nothing was hers save the gentle force of love. Yet through it she founded a spiritual empire that shall live after her, shall grow after her, and whose not slaved, but freed, subjects shall revere her memory forever.

✝

Peoria Journal, IL

The other day there passed away one of the most remarkable women of the past and present century. Her prototype has never been known in the history of the world.

She was the originator and the leader of a cult that is known all over the world, and that embraces in its membership some of the most intelligent people of this or any other nation. And therein it differs from any other cult of which we have any knowledge. Generally any movement like that of Christian Science takes in first the lower or at least the mediocre classes. The association of which Mrs. Eddy was the head took in the highest and the most intelligent.

Whatever may be said of Christian Science, there must be something about it to attract or such would not have been the case. There must have been something extraordinary about the head of that church, or she would not have attracted the clientage that she did. A few years ago there was an attempt made to "write down" Mrs. Eddy. It failed, and that was another demonstration of her great strength.

The sincerity of Mrs. Eddy has been questioned, but we have never entertained the least doubt that she was perfectly sincere in all that she said or did.

✠

Minneapolis Journal, MN

A leader to succeed Mrs. Eddy "never will be put forward," is the word unofficially emanating from the directors of The Mother Church in Boston. In this connection is recalled the fact that in 1895, Mrs. Eddy issued an order "ordaining" the Scriptures and her own *Science and Health* as "pastor" over The First Church of Christ, Scientist, in Boston, declaring that "they will continue to preach for this church and the world."

Higher criticism, so called, is supposed to have so far impeached for the majority of minds in this age the validity of a book as a medium through which God speaks, that the very props of the churches relying upon the book are considered by many to be broken. But here is a faith, new but as surely Christian in derivation and in sentiment as any Christian denomination or church, planting itself squarely on the written word, and considering that written word as so alive that it is spoken of as "pastor" and accepted as leader. A rather surprising commentary upon the alleged triumph of the higher criticism, to say the least! For Mrs.

Eddy's own work is held not as in the nature of a study and critical interpretation of the Scriptures, but as an inspired interpretation. Her interpretation is no more analogous to modern rationalistic criticism than are the institutes of Calvin. As Calvin, by those who heard and read him, was deemed something more than religious scholar and thinker, was felt to be inspired by the Spirit, and his interpretation of the Scriptures to share in the spiritual quality of those Scriptures, so the followers of Mrs. Eddy have conceived of her and her writings.

We are not here discussing the authenticity of Mrs. Eddy's inspiration, but merely noting its claim and its kind. It would seem that rationalism and science have no chance ever to persuade mankind that the Scriptures are history, literature, and legend, and that their spiritual worth is a matter of value and not of letter. It would seem as if every age interprets the Scriptures according to its vision, but that the Scriptures remain for many in every generation the inspired literal word.

Steamboat Pilot, Steamboat Springs, CO

Quietly, gently, with the halo and lovelight of a sublime faith that was triumphant over material ills, a noble woman has passed into new spheres of action, into a wider consciousness. Mary Baker Eddy is now being everywhere acclaimed as the most noble woman of history, and, as one paper says, through unnumbered generations and by countless millions of people she will be revered as the most inspired woman of all time.

When she first gave out her beautiful vision of the new faith which teaches the perfection of every living thing, of man made in the image and likeness of God, of a perfect creation, she was scoffed and ridiculed. She lived to be the leader of a million peaceful, happy souls and to be accorded a permanent place in the thought and action of the day by even those who do not accept her teachings. Through her message thousands of world-weary, pain-racked, and discouraged souls have been brought from darkness into light. Her story, which has been eagerly grasped by men and women in all parts of the world, tells of no death fear, of no sin or suffering, but of man as deathless, perfect, and eternal, the child of an infinite God, good. She has taught and found believers to the doctrine that the kingdom of heaven is not in some far-distant and mysterious land, but begins here, when man comes into harmony with his creator and manifests divine Love.

Coming into a materialistic age, she preached the doctrine of Spirit. Her mission was to banish grief and suffering, and the load she has lifted from human hearts entitles her to all the loving affection that she has received from her followers, and she has justly attained a fame that will be deathless. The whole world is seeking after truth. Thousands and hundreds of thousands believe, and have demonstrated to their satisfaction, that through Mrs. Eddy the truth has been revealed, and she has contributed in a greater measure than any other man or woman since Calvary to the sum total of human happiness.

Fairbanks Daily Times, Fairbanks, AK

The brief telegraphic announcement of the death of Mrs. Mary Baker Eddy, the Founder of Christian Science, will cause countless thousands to mourn. No woman ever lived who did more to strengthen faith and direct the footsteps of humanity toward the Master. Had Mrs. Eddy lived in the days when Jesus was on earth, she would have been a leader among the disciples, and like her Master would doubtless have been crucified. Living in later times, she has been crucified over and over again according to the modern method, which crucifies the spirit instead of the flesh. Openly reviled by the scoffers, she showed the same fortitude and forgiveness manifested by him, and like him, replied, "Father, forgive them; for they know not what they do."

The religion of Christian Science is so spiritual that many mortals are unable to follow it to all of its conclusions; but it is certain that all men can live and practise Christian Science in part, and they are benefited and uplifted in proportion as they are enabled to comprehend its Principle and apply it to the daily problems of life. Neither the Science nor the church will die with Mrs. Eddy, for it is founded on the rock. It may never become the universal religion, but it will go on and on, sustaining the faith and lifting millions of mortals up into a spiritual life that will benefit not only them but all mankind.

Knoxville Sentinel, TN

Mrs. Eddy was in her ninetieth year. Her old age had been serene and beautiful. Whatever may be the final word about her creed, its favorable influence on her own life can hardly be disputed. Mrs. Eddy suffered much from ill health until past the average of life. Her life-work began in 1866, when she was forty-five years of age, but it was ten years before the first Christian Science association was founded.

Mrs. Eddy has been a center of many controversies. It may be too early now to see her without partiality or prejudice, but few will deny that here was a unique personality, a buoyant courage, and an indomitable will. Her life differed from that of most noteworthy women. Its failures were in her youth, its successes were in her riper years. She found herself when approaching fifty. It was twenty years longer before she made the world admit her success. She will have no successor, for her position was that of a "founder."

Denver Republican, CO

In many respects a remarkable woman was Mrs. Eddy. She had tenacity of purpose, a genius for organization, and a belief in herself. She had a message to deliver, and that message has had a profound influence on the thought of to-day in this country. In her lifetime the Founder or revealer of this peculiarly woman's religion or dogma saw it grow to a numerical standard greater than any of this country's religious outgrowths, larger in membership and adherents than the Society of Friends or Quaker faith, with churches and practitioners in every civilized land. And it is not a militant religion; it wages no wars; it appeals to the average middle class more than to the extremist. It requires individual thought and study; to a considerable degree it is an individualistic religion.

Christian Science has brought a high standard in newspaper publication. It has demonstrated at least that there is a respectable minority abroad that relishes decent journalism. All in all, Mrs. Eddy has been a power for good. She inculcated gentleness in every-day life; she strove to abolish the "fear thought."

Decatur Herald, IL

Whatever may be the final estimate of the life of Mary Baker Eddy by those without the fold of the church which she established, it must be generally admitted that in many respects she was a remarkable woman. Relentlessly criticized and even persecuted as she was, assailed by the keenest minds and the sharpest intellects, her beliefs attacked and her theology condemned, she nevertheless maintained her prestige and saw her church grow from one small community of worshipers to thousands upon thousands. To-day Christian Science churches are represented in nearly every city in the land by stately edifices and loyal and devoted members. Mrs. Eddy had to a remarkable degree that ability as an organizer which is essential in any great undertaking. Once her church was established, she remained the recognized head of it.

She possessed a large amount of business acumen. This even her bitterest enemies stood willing to admit. Four years ago, when an attempt was being made to show that Mrs. Eddy was being unduly influenced by a "clique," a commission was sent to visit her at her Concord home. It was the report of this commission which largely influenced those behind the action to drop the case. Mrs. Eddy was then an elderly woman, who might have been expected to have lost touch with business matters, but her replies to questions as to how and why she invested her money, were worthy of the shrewdest banker. This is an age of tolerance, if not of the widest charity. Heretics no longer are burned, and we do not send to the rack those whose religious beliefs differ from our own. Mrs. Eddy's enemies have attacked her and attempted to ridicule *Science and Health,* but beyond declaring that her followers were strangely deluded they have had little to say regarding those who accepted her beliefs. She drew to her not only women, but men — men of great intellect, business men, scholars, men prominent in the professions, and in every one she found a defender.

It is probable that no leader or cause in history was ever more ably or systematically defended. Christian Science never antagonizes, but permits no statement against it to pass unquestioned. Its press system excites only admiration. It is altogether improbable that Mrs. Eddy's work will languish with her demise. It will be taken up by strong and willing hands and carried forward, and this the more easily for the reason that Mrs. Eddy had worked out her plans and left her house in order.

Beacon, Cannon Falls, MN

The tone of the press, as shown in editorial comments on the death of Mrs. Eddy, is a most encouraging indication of religious tolerance, as well as indicating the commanding position achieved by this teacher of righteousness. The attitude of the press in this instance shows plainly that any religious philosophy that has in it the elements of sincerity and of practical application to daily life, any religious belief or form that is helpful, is sure to be treated with toleration. It must, of course, stand the test of time to achieve permanent recognition as a distinct form, but toleration begins long before this point of recognition is reached. Mrs. Eddy's personality had perhaps something to do with the kindly expressions from every quarter of the globe on the occasion of her death, but the foundation of them was in nearly every instance the quality of her work. Mrs. Eddy's work and her philosophy of religion and of life is not as generally understood as we believe it should be, and we take pleasure in reproducing some of the many editorial comments that have come to hand touching her life and its influence on society. These excerpts are but samples of the wide-spread comment occasioned by the death of this great character, whom the world needs to know more intimately in order, that she may meet with deserved appreciation.

Register-Gazette, Rockford, IL

The world has lost a remarkable woman in the passing on of Mrs. Mary Baker Eddy. Not lost her entirely, however, for an individuality so pronounced as to gather nearly a million followers in a devotion which left no room for doubt of its sincerity, cannot vanish with the mere opening and closing of the gates which to so many of us separate the known from the unknown. Whatever the judgment as to the foundations on which she built, the general verdict of Mrs. Eddy's life must be a kindly one, for she taught helpfulness, sacrifice, and the inspiration that comes from one's own efforts; in brief, a very human doctrine of happiness. She possessed to a great degree brilliance of mind, temperamental strength, and poise. She found her way unerringly over many rough places and through deep shadows, and her light seemed to glow with greater radiance because of them. The responsibility of right thinking would seem a very approachable ground for mankind indeed, and this Mrs. Eddy has urged with a gentle insistence which undoubtedly has contributed much to the sum of the world's happiness. It is not easy to believe at this time that the church risen on her discovery will crumble; it is far easier to believe its faith is sufficiently established to safeguard it against all the failings of jealousy and ambition.

⚜

Quincy Herald, IL

The clarified judgment of history will be that the world has been made better and purer by the ministrations and example of the sweet-faced woman who was the Founder of the Christian Science church. Those who scoff at some of her tenets must admit that her teachings and writings have made for higher and better living — for clean manhood and womanhood and for a better moral, mental, and physical status of humanity. She has been much misunderstood, sometimes maligned, but was always kindly, patient, and pure. Those who refuse to accept her doctrines cannot but admit the beauty and stateliness of the language in which they are clothed. Purely for the wholesome serenity of its diction, and the immaculate virtue of its thought, her life-work, *Science and Health,* will have an eternal place in English literature.

⚜

Cleveland Press, OH

Mrs. Eddy triumphed over death long before she passed away. Any person who gives to the world enduring good triumphs over death. Whatever objection any one can present to some of the particular or peculiar claims of Christian Science, it is truth that Mrs. Eddy turned the thought and lives of thousands of people toward the divine sunshine, taught thousands to turn from the gloom of past errors, to close the door upon remorse, regret, disappointment, and failure, and look upon God as all good, all merciful, all Love. To do such is surely to triumph over death, even before the immaterial material body goes to the tomb.

Washington Herald, DC

Mrs. Mary Baker Eddy was unquestionably one of the most remarkable women of her time. She must have possessed unusual qualities to inspire so large a body of followers as she controlled; she must have had a remarkable mind in order to formulate a new doctrine which should prove sufficiently powerful to cause Christian Science churches to be erected in practically every city in the United States. But we are quite sure that the great secret of Mrs. Eddy's success lay in the sanity and reasonableness of the doctrines she promulgated.

World's Crisis, Boston, MA

The death of Mary Baker Eddy at her home near Boston was a recent event attracting wide-spread attention. As head of the Christian Science church, the latter part of her career has identified her with what must be considered, in many respects, the most remarkable religious movement of modern times. However much criticism she may have suffered at the hands of those not favorable to her system, there can be no doubt as to the loyalty and devotion of her followers.

Herald, Mexico City, Mexico

The general tone of the press in noticing the passing on of Mrs. Eddy is kindly and sympathetic. Many Jews have in the last few years become Christian Scientists, and the *American Israelite,* in noting the fact, praises Mrs. Eddy's tolerance toward non-believers in her teachings.

Worcester Telegram, MA

Mrs. Mary Baker Eddy leaves the largest personal following of any woman in American history, and perhaps in the world history. She has been for many years a conspicuous figure in New England life, and to-day is the most illustrious dead awaiting the formalities of burial, in all the world of civilization. It is the claim of her followers in the distinct creed she established that she is revered by more human beings than any other known to modern life, and that her teachings and example have raised them to higher and more intelligent thought and method of living. It has never been disputed that her students have been enlisted from among the best products of civilization, and it is not at all improbable that they have improved by the tendency to concentrate their thoughts upon the new ideals. They have thus formed for themselves a new environment, and they have not been ungenerous in shedding their light among the people with whom they have come in contact in the activities of the world.

With all its faults as often mentioned in human converse and fought in various ways by opponents, it is to the credit of Christian Science that it has never used fear of a deity as one of its supporting pillars before the public. That at least gives it a high standing among the doctrines that have been spread before mankind in many ages, and in that one respect the highest. It may be said to have banished that condition of the mind from millions, and even with that accomplishment it has benefited the world. It may be the highest tribute that mankind can offer to the memory of one woman that she banished fear from their religions.

But the work that has been done among many people by the Christian Science organization is greater even than that. It has builded without fighting to destroy the good effects of other building. Nowhere has this Science taught or practiced war, nowhere upheld war or any other form of slaughter of human life or character. Peace for all nations and conditions of people, and without sacrifice of principle or inherent right, is one of the tenets of the Science that formed the foundation for the organization, and it has thus far operated without making a class or pitting one existing class against another.

Its growth as a church, as a public order element, is noteworthy, and its growth as a beautifier of the living places of men is no less to its credit. And always as an organization it holds the strongest place, without having called forth public criticism because of methods of oppression in the monopoly of any article the people needed as an established necessity. It has presented a clean slate and a clean character, personal as well as in organization. It is an outgrowth of modern development, with less of the harking back to the dark ages than some others, and much if not all of that must be said to have been the result of mental efforts of Mrs. Eddy. Her long life was lived for a greater purpose than she has been given credit for in this material-istic age.

Springfield Republican, MA

Judged by her achievement, Mrs. Mary Baker Eddy was one of the extraordinary figures of the nineteenth century. It is difficult to present any estimate of her career without inviting controversy, and now that she is dead controversy will flame up again, as her work is freshly studied. For it is certain that her life was a marvel. It was a career from which every one may draw immense inspiration, further-more. It is the inspiration that must come from the specta-cle of astonishing achievement brought about by a woman whose whole life up to the age of fifty had been an utter failure, as the world viewed it and as many of her most in-timate acquaintances estimated it. One may search history from the beginning and have difficulty in matching Mrs. Eddy's performance, between the ages of fifty and eighty, in making a million people accept her at her own valua-tion. No one can read the story of her career and say that a life which seems the dreariest of futilities in middle age may not contain the possibilities of large achievement in the remaining years. For the part played by circumstances in affording the requisite opportunity for the development of a remarkable personality was never more vividly shown than in this woman's late unfolding as the Leader of what is known as Christian Science.

Mrs. Eddy must be credited also with having done good. Whether or not the church she founded long survives her death, whether or not her system of healing the sick retains any considerable number of adherents, it must be said that she served a useful purpose in organizing an effective protest against the defective methods of the old schools of medicine and in forcing upon the attention of men of science as well as upon the multitude that careful consideration which the purely psychic element in disease so much deserves.

The criticism of Mrs. Eddy and of Christian Science, which is her monument, may be found in many books. At this time it is proper to recognize the dimensions of her practical achievement and the claims which her remarkably complex and subtle yet most forceful personality have upon the world's attention and regard.

Milwaukee Free Press, WI

Whatever may be the ultimate fate of Christian Science, whether it continues to wax in power and spiritual fruitage or eventually becomes absorbed or superseded in the religious evolution of mankind, Mrs. Eddy is assured of a permanent niche in that great gallery of seers and interpreters who have made clear the way of God to man. The most vital history of the human race is ever its religious history, and no chronicles of the epoch-making evolution that has taken place in the conception and attitude of man toward the divinity, during the past three decades, can possibly leave out of account the teachings and the ministry of Mrs. Eddy.

One need not be a believer in Christian Science, one need not even be an admirer of its Founder, to appreciate this and to acknowledge this. For, remarkable as has been the achievement of this remarkable woman in giving renewed and beneficent potency to an ancient revelation, remarkable as has been her administration in building up a powerful church, both materially and spiritually, her achievement does not stop there. The influence of Christian Science has extended far beyond the confines of its church or the bounds of its adherents; it has in its essential spirit proved a leavening force both in other churches and among masses who confess to no faith or creed. Mrs. Eddy was ready with her interpretation of the Scriptures when the desire for a more immanent and spiritual conception of the Christian God began to stir the heart and mind of America, and in the great liberating, spiritualizing movement in religious thought that grew out of this, Christian Science has played its unquestioned part. It profited from this movement, to be sure, but in turn it also proved a source of sustenance.

The man or woman who has been healed in body or soul through Christian Science will naturally cherish a peculiar devotion for the author of this faith and its practice. While the significance and beauty of this phase of Mrs. Eddy's work need not be underestimated, the chances are that with the larger understanding of psychic healing which is rapidly coming to pass, the author of *Science and Health* will be celebrated less because of the therapeutic element in her teachings than for their aid in bringing about a closer, more spiritual, and efficacious communion between man and his Maker.

New Haven Journal-Courier, CT

There will be three judgments entered with regard to the character and life of Mary Baker Eddy, the Founder of the Christian Science church. By her large following she will be worshiped as a saint. By another large group of open-minded men and women she will be viewed as an extraordinary person, who possessed great spiritual insight and executive genius. By a smaller and more intolerant group, she will be condemned.

It is of little interest to us what the attitude of this third class is or may be. We have found it difficult to accept at its full face value the leadership of this remarkable woman. We have found it easy to accept her in the light the second group has accepted her. She has built up a church which has shown marvelous growth, and she has welcomed into it thousands of people of the highest personal character and spiritual earnestness. Others in this free country are at liberty to make what use they like of the activities and convictions of their neighbors as they relate to Christian professions. The mysteries of life, the magic of the beginning and the pall of its close, have not so revealed themselves to our eyes that they appear easy of analysis when applied to any given religious faith. They are rather so profound in their elusiveness that that form of belief which brings peace of mind and contentment of soul to its followers, compels our respectful consideration, at least, by whatever title it is known.

Battle Creek Daily Moon, MI

If history makes clear any one fact, it is that contemporaneous judgments often are inaccurate. The perspective of time is necessary to a calm analysis of the influences which shape thought. Posterity more than once has rejected those acclaimed prophets in a bygone day, and crowned those who were overlooked by their fellows. The axiom will hold good in the case of Mrs. Mary Baker Eddy, Discoverer and Founder of Christian Science. The world is too close to her life and her work to give an unbiased decision as to her significance. On the one hand are her thousands of followers, scattered in almost every civilized land, who believe she has given to the world a real message of peace, hope, and ultimate freedom from the ills to which flesh so long has been heir. On the other hand are her many critics, some bitter, some mild, but all denying her doctrines.

The storm of controversy which has raged about Mrs. Eddy personally and as the Leader of a faith, is not likely to cease at her death. It is predicted on one side that the church which she has founded will topple and fall without the cohesive influence of her captaincy, and, on the other, that she put it on its feet long ago and that it will move forward on its own momentum. Whatever the future has to tell of Mrs. Eddy and her teaching, and aside from whatever opinion one may have as to the tenets she preached, it is certain that she has been a powerful factor in current thought. The growth of Christian Science as the sincere belief of men and women of varied classes, the hundreds of magnificent churches which have been reared by her disciples, and, most of all, the enormous circulation of her book, *Science and Health with Key to the Scriptures,* proves this.

If any one influence which she exerted should be remembered, it is that she taught optimism. Christian Scientists are sunny, hopeful, cheerful. The Leader taught that brooding on the ills of life is a sin, and this wholesome doctrine has remade chronic grumblers and fretful invalids, loaded under a burden of imaginary ills, into bright, active, and helpful men and women.

Evening Journal, Wilmington, DE

Mrs. Mary Baker Eddy may be regarded without exaggeration as the most remarkable woman of her time. Her hold upon her followers was indeed wonderful. In a day when all questions of a religious nature are subjected to the most critical tests, when some boast that the statements and influences of men of regular science have great weight and tend to demolish religious theories and principles of the past, Mrs. Eddy founded a religious denomination which has grown and prospered in a very remarkable manner. Her adherents have been and are of a type of high intelligence. She has never been strong among what may be called the masses of the people, and in this Christian Science differs from any of the other religious sects which have been founded but which have gained their first adherents among what are termed the more lowly. Indeed Christianity itself had such a beginning, as the disciples, nearly all of them, were not from the wealthy or the aristocratic or the ruling classes.

One thing evident about the true Christian Scientists, which shows the powerful and beneficial influence that Mrs. Eddy has exerted in the world, is that they are firm in the faith, energetic and relentless in upholding it, and to all outward appearances in their lives are most happy. The religion founded by Mrs. Eddy has brought peace to many a distressed soul. After all, what higher benefit could it confer?

Commercial News, Danville, IL

The passing of Mrs. Eddy removes from the world one of the most remarkable women of modern times. She was the Leader of a religious movement which has greatly impressed the world, and which attracted more than a million followers to her. For the past quarter of a century she was the Leader of the movement which revolutionized her followers, their thoughts, and their methods of living. She believed in healing and saving power by divine right. She never preached that there is no material death, although she has predicted the ultimate conquest of death in time to come. There need be no difficulty in the minds of Christian Scientists in reconciling the physical fact of her death with their disbelief in death itself.

Her work will continue. Her church will continue to live of its own momentum. She placed it on such an enduring basis that it can guide itself. She can have no successor, because no one can do the work she has done. Mrs. Eddy was a great leader. When there was dissension in her church, she proved what she was capable of by sweeping away all opposition. Her followers had faith in her which was almost sublime. When she has been dead a century men and women will better understand her work and her worth than they do at the present time. Her death removes one of the greatest figures of our day.

Rich Hill Daily Review, MO

By the "passing on" of Mrs. Mary Baker Eddy there will be profound sorrow in the hearts of many thousands of good people on earth, but no mourning by her immediate followers, or at least no outward sign thereof. Whatever the opinion of those who could not accept Mrs. Eddy's theories either in a religious or rational sense, the fact remains that as the Discoverer and Founder of Christian Science, aside from all the rest of her life-work, she was one of the most remarkable and powerful women of the age.

To have possessed the will-power and ability to establish a cult or religion in a single generation that could beget the following of intelligent and cultured people which Christian Science has, not only in this country but in other lands, is a remarkable thing in itself, and in other ages would have been regarded as almost superhuman. Yet this achievement has been wrought by this woman from a very humble beginning, and to-day thousands of churches and schools have been established to teach and perpetuate this faith — and among them some of the finest religious edifices in the land — and hundreds and thousands of followers, embracing some of the best people morally, and some of the wealthiest citizens, are enlisted in the work begun by Mrs. Eddy.

The foundation upon which Mrs. Eddy based her structure, viz., that mind predominates matter, has been recognized among the philosophers of the past ages; but it was left to her to systematize this vague truth and to develop and expand it, and to extend it far beyond any hitherto recognized limit. How well she has succeeded must be judged by the number, the character, and the fidelity of her followers. Whether her system has been fully perfected, whether there must be additions thereto or modifications thereof, still remains to be seen. Whether her theories appeal to us who are not among her votaries, or however irrational they may seem to us, Mrs. Eddy has made a wonderful demonstration in the last few decades of her lifetime, and all must accredit her with a wonderful force and power.

St. Louis Times, MO

It will be conceded very widely that with the death of Mrs. Eddy one of the most remarkable women of the age has passed away. A woman with the will and power to establish, in the period of a few decades, a religion, or cult, and place it upon an apparently unshakable foundation, must possess more than ordinary powers. The growth of the Christian Science movement, the establishment of churches in magnificent buildings, and the organization of hundreds of thousands of people in a faith which has become world-wide — this has been one of the extraordinary phenomena of the present and the past centuries.

Those of materialistic tendencies, and those who adhere to the simpler faiths, may withhold approval of what this woman achieved. But just as certainly there will be many thousands who will regard her as a genuine benefactor — a real healer.

Athens Daily Messenger, OH

Whatever one's theory about Christian Science, the career of Mrs. Eddy, who recently passed out in her ninetieth year, is without a parallel. At forty years of age, a confirmed invalid, she somehow came into possession of a power that made her into a healthy woman, and she so analyzed and systemized that power and set it forth in a wonderfully able book of philosophy on Christianity, that others are able to get her thought and use it for a broader life of health and happiness and freedom from dogmatism and creed, jealousies and hate. Her philosophy of life has been adopted by over a million followers in the civilized world, and Christian Science is to-day one of the most rapidly growing Christian organizations in the world.

The ideas of Christian Science are old, dating back before Christ, and the Founder maintained that the power of Jesus and his disciples to heal the sick is a living and universal power, everlasting and eternal, but for centuries lost to Christians. It remained for Mrs. Eddy to rediscover this power and reduce it to what she and her followers call a Science, — that is, a rational and demonstrable proposition.

Albert Lea Tribune, MN

The death of Mrs. Mary Baker Eddy, the Christian Science Leader, removes from our midst one of the most remarkable figures of late years. A woman said to be possessed of the most lovable qualities, she exercised a tremendous influence upon the lives of thousands of people, not only in this country, but in different parts of the world. Whether we agree with her and accept her teachings or not, we must certainly admire those qualities about her which brought her to the forefront among the women and men of the day, and made her one of the leading persons of the world.

La Crosse Tribune, WI

It would be unwise for one not thoroughly conversant with Christian Science to attempt discourse upon the life-work of Mary Baker Eddy. Criticism of her creed has been bitter in some quarters, and she has been frequently denounced as an imposter. But no one now attempts to deny that she was one of the most powerful and most remarkable women in history. Her works are a monument to these things. She achieved wonderful success, and that she leaves behind her more than one hundred thousand followers whose confidence is implicit, is a fact calculated to rebuke sweeping accusations against her.

Jerseyman, Morristown, NJ

Mary Baker Eddy, the Founder and Leader of the cult of Christian Scientists, was, in some respects, the most notable personage of the century. Whatever views may be held in regard to this belief, it cannot be disputed that its followers generally are of the cultured class, and they find in it that which gives serenity of mind and an optimistic spirit that suggests a life in that beatific land of the prophet's vision, the inhabitant of which shall not say, "I am sick."

Times, San Juan, Puerto Rico

The Christian Science church has lost its Founder in the death of Mary Baker Eddy — the most powerful religious leader of this age, and a woman who reached that position through a new interpretation of the Bible. Her appeal was made primarily to the sick and infirm, and "Life, Truth, and Love are all powerful and ever present" was her text. Regardless of the merits or demerits of Christian Science, the fact remains that it has a large and influential following, that its members are earnest and intelligent men and women, and that it has gained its following by appeal to the reason rather than through force and persecution.

Never before in history has a woman founded so important a movement.

Denver Post, CO

Mrs. Mary Baker Eddy, Founder and Leader of the Christian Science church, has gone to her reward. She needs no tears, no sobs, no grief. Her spirit has earned eternal rest, and has departed to claim its wage. This woman stood behind a new church, a new belief, a new creed. By her teachings she brought ease and quiet to many a tired, worn-out body, contentment to many a weary heart, and peace to many a soul in distress. If that be all she ever did, then her work was well done; but there was more, oh, so much more! She started out alone. She gathered around her a little circle. They believed — with her. The enthusiasm spread, until finally thousands — millions — were ready to embrace the teaching that brought joy and happiness, and nothing else.

Mrs. Eddy raised up an institution — and supported it — which promulgates the beautiful thought that every human being is graven in the image of its God, and that there is no evil in the world except that which has grown into the hearts of the people of the earth. Cast out that evil — according to her — and nothing but bliss remains. Take away the bickerings and revilings which have been the Christian Scientist's lot; forget the attacks to which he has been subjected, and you still have left a Principle that has aided a world to higher and better things. It teaches of a glorious world to come, where tired souls will find a safe haven. It tells of a hereafter where spirits worn from the world's strife will find eternal happiness. It depicts another existence that we should all be glad to go to. It whispers of no death fear; it voices no sick-bed alarm; it dismisses belief in bodily ailments; it cries that the world is good, that all is beautiful, that there is no wrong or evil except that which we ourselves create. Without argument, without defense, taken merely as an abstract proposition, the thought is exquisite. It has brought the smile to many a worn face, ease to many a body in pain, and contentment to many a sore-tried heart.

The church this woman reared will live on. Others will rise up to take her place. Many will continue the work which one had done before. But, remember, just as she taught there should be no grief in the world, she wants none now that she is gone. It came her time to go, and she went with the knowledge she was but journeying to the things she had laid up for herself in another world. If she could speak to-day, she would say to all her followers: "Let there be no heartaches."

Herald-Democrat, Leadville, CO

It is not every generation that is permitted to witness the passing of the founder of a religion, nor is it every generation that produces such a unique character. In fact, the history of the world furnishes comparatively few individuals with the peculiar qualifications needed to lead a great movement of a spiritual character, and away from the orthodox standards of the period in which they lived.

Mrs. Eddy will probably stand alone in some respects. There have been great women teachers and leaders, women notable in every walk of life, but no woman has ever before actually founded and established a powerful religious sect, and has so guided and directed its energies that its adherents are now numbered by the hundreds of thousands and its material wealth counted by the millions, and which is recognized by students of religious phenomena as one of the most remarkable manifestations of the kind the world has ever seen.

Mrs. Eddy makes the Bible the basis of her teachings. Herself an educated woman and a student of what science calls ultimate problems, or as it is termed metaphysics, she evolved that remarkable combination, the uniting of a difficult metaphysical abstraction, namely, the non-existence of matter and the reality of mind, with deep religious feeling. The philosophers had been disputing for centuries about mind and matter, good and evil, pain and pleasure. Mrs. Eddy boldly seized on a single proposition — God is all good, therefore there can be no evil, hence the things called evil are figments and imaginings of mortal mind — and a new religion appeared.

It appealed to thousands in the midst of the American civilization of the nineteenth century, because it offered to accomplish a definite purpose in this world, namely, the healing of disease. It won its converts, as all religions have won theirs, by demonstrations of its ability to cure, for no one can deny the fact that there have been cures accomplished.

Lebanon Western Star, OH

Mrs. Mary Baker Eddy, the organizer of the Christian Science church, is dead, or — as the adherents of that faith more beautifully say — has passed from among us. In leaving this world, she leaves it the richer because of her life and her teachings.

We are not a member of that church, but for it we have worlds of commendation, just as we have for all branches of the church and all organizations, under whatever title they are living, that seek to alleviate pain and sorrow, whether physical, mental, or spiritual, and thus make this old world better. It is our pleasure to know many members of the Christian Science church, and it is also a great pleasure to say that — judged by the standards by which the world judges Christians — every one of them is leading a more worthy life than was led before accepting that belief. This might have been true had they united with any other church — we are not seeking an argument, simply stating a fact.

Current Literature

The column on column of news despatches and editorial comment evoked by the death of Mary Baker Eddy, the Founder of Christian Science, may be said to reveal an important change in the psychology of this country. America, it is clear, is beginning to take Mrs. Eddy and her doctrines seriously. Where in past years bitter intolerance and a disposition to regard her as a charlatan have existed, the prevailing spirit is now one of interested inquiry. "Whatever the degree of faith or unfaith with which the individual may look upon what she taught and what was accomplished by or through her teachings," says the *Chicago Tribune,* in a mood that is almost universal, she was "one of the most remarkable women of her time." The *New York World* goes farther in characterizing her as "perhaps the most extraordinary woman of her century."

Seattle Daily Times, WA

Mary Baker Eddy is dead — and in her death one of the most interesting characters of modern times has passed away. Even an "unbeliever" must pay tribute to the force and influence of this wonderful woman. There are those who scoff at her death — claiming that she taught the doctrine that there was no such thing as death; but it will be remembered that there have been those in all times who have scoffed at those who could not verify in realism the theories of an ideal. This is not intended as a discussion of Christian Science in any of its phases. We are treating of the woman herself, rather than of anything which she taught or sought to teach.

Christian Science to-day is known all over the world, and it is safe to say that this fact is due almost entirely to the work of this wonderful woman. There are at least only two or three persons in a century of the history of the world who have developed such a following as this aged woman commanded. Most women, in similar conditions, would have arrogated to themselves a sort of regal authority and regal splendor. But this woman lived simply and quietly — not in poverty — not in luxury — but in comfort. Her pleasures were few and her wants — not many. Offered almost idolatry by some of her followers, she accepted little in the way of homage, and what she did accept she accepted rather as a vindication of her teachings than as a tribute to her personality. And yet it will be as a "personality" that at least the "unbelieving" world will remember her at the present. She was a wonderful woman!

Lima Times-Democrat, OH

Whatever may have been said in opposition to the teachings of Mrs. Mary Baker Eddy, by authorities in other religious denominations, it must be admitted that her followers are the cheeriest lot of optimists, as a whole, there are in the world to-day. They look upon the bright side of everything, and they see and know no evil. There is no room in them or among them for the man or woman who thinks evil. For that, if for nothing else, the Founder of The Mother Church should be and will be called blessed. It isn't a bad sort of a religion that, which makes people look on the bright side always, and forever and continuously instils the doctrine of love.

There is something more than ordinary in a life that by example and teaching has remade many chronic grumblers and fretful invalids into bright, active, and helpful men and women. There is something in a life which, in the face of aconstant storm of controversy, such as has raged about Mrs. Eddy, can bring to it growing thousands of devotees of all classes, each with sincere belief in the truth of Christian Science. There is some wonderful force behind a life that can cause the building of hundreds of magnificent places for worship.

At this near view of the work of Mrs. Eddy it is certain she has given to thousands and thousands a message of peace, hope, and ultimate freedom from the ills that have been their lot. What the future judgment may be, only the perspective of time as a calm analyst of the influences which shape thought can determine. Anyhow, the world is better, much better, that Mrs. Eddy lived.

Lowell Courier-Citizen, MA

The death — for let us speak as the world's people do — of Mrs. Mary Baker Eddy, head of the Christian Science church and Leader of that sect, will receive wide notice in due proportion to the importance of the position of this remarkable woman in the world of affairs. Of all the variants on the theme of the Christian religion, hers is the only one of very recent years which has attained to world-wide magnitude. Differing from other denominations of Christians in its attitude toward the visitations of disease and frequently misunderstood even there, it has achieved an uncommon degree of attention. Judged by the purely pragmatic theory, it must be acknowledged to have made its way and to have assured its position, at least for the present generation. That which, in its day, actually gives to its adherents comfort and joy in this world and a hope of the life everlasting in the world to come, is entitled on those merits alone to share in making up the "true" religion of mankind. All that helps has its place.

Whether one follows Mrs. Eddy's peculiar teachings or not as they affect certain details of her faith, it must be admitted that she set before men and women of the materialistic nineteenth and twentieth centuries a system of belief that has afforded to many hundred thousand much practical comfort and hope. Whether or not the practices of Christian Science, in the healing of the thousand natural shocks the flesh is heir to, or its maintenance of a belief as to the non-existence of pain and suffering for one in whom a proper frame of mind is induced by faith, are justifiable on the basis of actual science, the fact must remain undisputed that for such as do believe in them there has been a remarkable force.

Tuscaloosa News, AL

The passing of Mrs. Mary Baker Eddy removes from the world one of the most remarkable women of the last and present century, if not of all time. Practically all other religions or sects of religions have had at their head men, although women have always played a large part in upholding them and spreading their influence. Mrs. Eddy stands alone among women as a great religious teacher.

Regardless of the sanity of the doctrines of Mrs. Eddy, one cannot but acknowledge the power of mind and personality that enabled her to build up a powerful church. From a very simple beginning, Mrs. Eddy worked and studied constantly until to-day her followers are numbered by thousands and the property which the church owns is valued at millions. But Mrs. Eddy was not merely a religious worker in the narrow sense of the word. She not only gave her best thought to what she considered the spiritual and bodily needs of the world, but also contributed generously in money to philanthropic movements and to civic improvements. All in all, the ninety years of her life were well spent, for she no doubt brought both spiritual satisfaction and bodily comfort into many homes.

Telegraph, New London, CT

It is not our province to dwell upon the significance to Christian Scientists of the passing of their beloved Leader. Suffice it to say that while her departure is felt in sorrow and regret, her followers have no fear that the loss of her physical presence is to deprive them of the fruits of her life-work, nor will there be any attempt or tendency upon their part to deify her human personality, understanding her teaching to forever condemn idolatry. As a religious leader Mrs. Eddy is unique. History affords no parallel. The world accords to her the distinction of having been the most remarkable woman of her time, and for the most part is content that the truth or falsity of her teaching shall be tested by time and by its fruits rather than by the rules of logic or of orthodoxy.

Times-Record, Fort Smith, AR

Whatever one's views as to Mrs. Eddy's teachings, she must be accorded rank as one of the greatest intellectual forces of the world's history. She won this distinction through the usual adverse influences which must be overcome by any one who advances a thought out of the beaten, well-trodden path — namely, ridicule, slander, calumny, and a persecution no less cruel for that it was not physical. Beginning with a handful of student followers, to-day the principle which she advanced is taught in approximately a thousand churches in this and other lands, many of them of the most costly and beautiful architecture. To have accomplished this in the span of one life, to see the humble beginning and the wonderful spread of one's thought, is something given to few mortals. Besides this, Mrs. Eddy had the satisfaction of knowing that the acceptance of her thought and interpretation of the Word of God had brought the blessing of health to many thousands sick in mind, heart, and body. This reapplication of the divine injunction to heal the sick through the teachings of Christ, although for many years it subjected her and her followers to ridicule and opposition, has at last, by its demonstration of truth, aroused the emulation of the older established sects so that they are seriously considering the formal recognition of a long neglected practice of the early Christian faith.

Day, New London, CT

Mrs. Eddy certainly was a remarkable woman. She had the faculty of leading others, and the success of the movement that she originated is the greatest monument that could be reared to her memory. The growth of Christian Science has been one of the wonders of recent times, and the fact that it prospered in spite of the most violent opposition and abuse shows that there was something about it that appealed to the intelligence of its devotees, for it has attracted men and women of notable intellectual ability.

Phoenix Democrat, AZ

Probably no person during this century was subjected to a greater degree of criticism than was this patient, silent woman. While we are not wholly familiar with the teachings of Mrs. Eddy, yet we realize that she has accomplished a great work in her lifetime; and to-day probably not another individual in all this great country will be more sincerely mourned.

The charge that Mrs. Eddy was rich — that her gifts were utilized for the accumulation of wealth — is not well taken. Her wealth came from a grateful people; came from a grand army of men and women who loved their teacher for the benefits that came to them through her teachings. During the last forty years Mrs. Eddy has probably brought more sunshine into the homes of the poor — instilled more hope into the sinking, tired hearts of ailing humanity — than any one person in the last century. Her life was devoted to the uplifting of humanity; and, be her teachings as they may, hundreds of thousands of intelligent men and women will to-day drop a tear in kind and loving remembrance.

***

Portland Express and Advertiser, ME

Through years of misunderstanding and misrepresentation, Mary Baker Eddy, the Discoverer and Founder of Christian Science, went serenely and confidently on with the work she believed herself called to do. She lived to see her faith adopted in many lands, to see beautiful and costly church edifices erected in many cities, both in America and abroad, lovingly dedicated to her and to her teachings. Only forty years have passed since she stood alone, the only exponent of her faith in all the world. To-day thousands rise up and call her blessed, and in the Wednesday evening meetings of the denomination, clouds of witnesses testify weekly to the power of divine Love, as she taught of it, to heal from sickness and from sin. These followers constitute the monument to her memory which must most have contributed to her joy. Mrs. Eddy's place in history is secure. Her adherents are living examples of a vital faith. The church she founded holds an important place in the religious world. The voice of detraction should now be forever silenced.

News-Democrat, Canton, OH

The death of Mary Baker Eddy, the Founder of Christian Science, has closed the earthly career of one of the most marvelous women of modern times, if not of all time. That she was a profoundly good woman, teaching a gospel of truth and love, will be universally admitted. That the influence of her teachings — the philosophy she preached and practised — has been tremendous, must be acknowledged. Measured by the results it has accomplished for the thousands and tens of thousands of men and women who, understanding it and believing it, have made it a rule of their life, its potentiality cannot be doubted.

While the passing away of Mrs. Eddy has brought a sense of sorrow to her devoted followers, they insist that the church will not perish, but continue its growth, and the philosophy of Christian Science will be as enduring as time itself. Be that as it may, the death of Mary Baker Eddy removes from earth a woman of whom it can be said, The world has been made immeasurably better because she lived in it.

Coshocton Daily Age, OH

The passing of Mrs. Mary Baker Eddy removes one of the world's great women, no matter whether one agreed with her teachings or not. She filled her place in the world and filled it well. Her teachings, no matter what else they may maintain, worked for purity, honesty, and temporal concord, as well as the ever betterment of self. She held undoubted power over those who followed her faith, but mature study of conditions leads an outsider to believe it was the power of love rather than the power of fear. With a wonderful equanimity she withstood the bitterest assaults, and was an embodiment of the Biblical adage that "a soft answer turneth away wrath."

Pueblo Indicator, CO

Mrs. Eddy is dead, but Christian Science did not die with her, and thereby is unfolded a tale of more stability than many supposed the cult possessed, for this remarkable woman was its originator, its Founder, and for long years one of its chiefest supporters. And now that she is gone, that the gospel which she expounded still remains is to be taken as one of the proofs that Christian Science is based upon something substantial. It must be that it affords great spiritual comfort and consolation, else so many men and women of high intelligence and well known good citizenship would not belong to that sect.

The Farmers Voice, Chicago, IL

Not merely one of the world's great women — one of the world's great personages passed away when Mary Baker Eddy died in Boston. She must be adjudged great if measured only by the extent of the influence she exerted over the minds and lives of men and women over all the earth. That influence was world-wide and strongly potent in its workings, guiding and controlling the views of hundreds upon hundreds of thousands of exceptionally intelligent disciples.

Temple Daily Telegram, TX

In the day in which a religion is born but few people realize it, and it takes generations usually to develop a following for great teachers. In Mrs. Eddy's case she lived to see her church and her doctrines adopted by millions, and who knows but that in the distant future those who knew her and were her companions will be held in the same veneration as are to-day the disciples of Christ, whose teachings she illuminated?

✖️

Yorkshire Evening Post, Leeds, England

No one (says a writer in the *Outlook*) ever entered Mrs. Eddy's study who did not leave it not only a braver but a better man.

✖️

News-Signal, Middletown, OH

One of the remarkable characters not well understood by the world at large was Mary Baker Eddy. Her religious zeal, her claims, and her work would make a good subject for a sermon. In the first place, she built up a larger following than any other woman who has ever lived has built up. It has been given only to men in the past to become leaders of large classes of people, the organizations founded upon the teachings of women having always been limited in numbers.

In the next place, it is doubtful if any other person has lived in modern times who has had a more loyal following, those professing the doctrines she taught not only making those doctrines a part of their daily lives, but passing to eternity without fear of the future while embracing them. In other words, they have found Christian Science not only a religion by which to live, but also a religion which comforted in the last hours. In no other church to-day is there more implicit faith than in the Christian Science church, and that faith is centered in the words of this one woman and her interpretation of the Scriptures.

Arizona Journal-Miner, Prescott, AZ

The average intelligence of Christian Scientists ranks far ahead of the intelligence of any other creedal membership, and in its ranks are found many talented and intellectual people. It is only the uninformed who attempt to deny these facts. To have founded such a faith, whether it lasts ten or a thousand years after her death, is a wonderful and glorious work. They who did not know Mrs. Eddy personally have no means of judging her save by her work, and this was only good. She found a large body of intelligent, broad-minded, unorthodox men and women, who still demanded a set and limited religious belief, and she gave them one the like of which the history of the world has never seen. She found ailing, nervous, and diseased men and women who, being unable to cure their own ills, were as unsuccessful in securing health from orthodox sources, and she healed them — thousands of them. Only the uninformed will care to deny it. Mrs. Eddy was in many respects the most remarkable figure in all the nineteenth century and in the first decade of the twentieth.

Index-Republican, Bellefontaine, OH

One of the most remarkable women of the age, or of any age, has ended her career in the death of the Founder of Christian Science. The most bitter hostility to Mrs. Eddy and the most complete rejection of her doctrines and her church organization cannot, if honest and intelligent, deny that she has been a far-reaching and vital force in the thought and life of her times. The religion which she founded and completely dominated has more or less colored and permeated very important phases of existence for a multitude of men and women who do not call themselves Christian Scientists and are not, in fact, connected with the Christian Science organization.

Westmount News, Quebec

The world has had many women of great deeds, and among the modern women of achievement and fame not one has stood with us and approached nearer the zenith of her hopes than Mrs. Mary Baker Eddy. We in Westmount do not know as much as we should of the Christian Science movement, but although it has hardly passed its thirtieth mile-stone its power and influence is being greatly felt. Across the border, from The Mother Church in Boston, have gone forward crusaders with stout hearts, and to-day there are over one thousand branches, scattered across two continents.

News Scimitar, Memphis, TN

Mrs. Eddy's text-book, *Science and Health with Key to the Scriptures,* accepted the statements of the Bible that God made all, and all He made was good; that He was Spirit; and then concluded that, being Spirit, He could create nothing so unlike Himself as matter, and further, He being Spirit, man made in His likeness and image must be spiritual. She also rested her case on the other statement that God, while all wise, all powerful, and all present, was of purer vision than to behold evil, and she contended that evil was only a lie from the father of lies, a negation, the absence or denial of good, or maybe ignorance of good.

Mrs. Eddy's church, in the forty years of her ministry and leadership, probably grew faster than any other religious body in the same time, and it is a monument to her that its membership embraces people of culture and of the best type of citizenship, in the ordinary affairs of life. As to her doctrine or her interpretation of the Scriptures, it is difficult to see how her carrying the inconsequence of the material to the ultimate of its actual non-existence, could be other than helpful to civilization, as all wars, large or small, between different nations, or the frictions of individuals, are over the possession and enjoyment of the material, because in the world of Spirit there is no limitation or lack. One man's unlimited possessions in the field of Spirit in no sense diminish any other man's possessions. On the material plane, every man's holdings in some degree diminish other men's holdings.

Mrs. Eddy finally won her way to the respect of the country, of the world, among believers and non-believers particularly, so far as this could be learned from expressions of the press. As to the attitude of her following, probably no other leader has attained such distinction of unqualified deference and influence, not only on their professions and outer conduct, but on their lives.

Daily Times, Leavenworth, KS

Whatever condemnation or praise may be accorded the creed of Christian Science — and it receives its meed of both — Mary Baker Eddy in giving it to the world performed a worthy service. Christian Science, putting aside any discussion of its specific tenets, teaches right living, and any instruction which encourages us to live wholesome lives, even according to lay judgments is good. The creed, enlisting some of the best minds in the country, must by that very evidence, have a preponderance of virtue in it, a quality which Mrs. Eddy supplied.

Ottawa Daily Republic, KS

The death of Mrs. Mary Baker Eddy removes from the arena of human activity one of the brightest and strongest minds that the world has produced. Believers in the doctrines of Christian Science revere Mrs. Eddy as almost divine, while unbelievers are compelled to acknowledge the force of her wonderful personality. The Founder of a new religious system who can in a single generation mold the thought and win the allegiance of nearly a million intelligent people must be accorded credit for exceptional genius. This Mrs. Eddy did. She established a religious society noted the world over for its sincerity and zeal, and one which, in all probability, will be a monument to her name for many generations to come.

Marshalltown Daily Herald, IA

The death of Mrs. Mary Baker Eddy has removed from life perhaps the most unique woman character known to history. This much may be truthfully said, and there are none who are familiar with the church she founded who will question this, whether her doctrines appeal to them or not. The fact stands out clearly that her teachings have taken hold in a most remarkable way on the lives of many thousands of people, and these people are among the very best in the country.

Success Magazine

The Christian Science church has lost its Founder and Leader in the death of Mary Baker Eddy — the most powerful religious leader of this age, and a woman who reached that position through a new interpretation of the Bible. Regardless of the merits or demerits of Christian Science, the fact remains that it has a large and influential following, that its members are earnest and intelligent men and women, and that it has gained its following by appeal to the reason rather than through force and persecution. Never before in history has a woman founded so important a movement.

Parsons Sun, KS

The death of Mrs. Mary Baker Eddy removes from life one who has blessed life in the living. She gave to the world a new creed and a new guide of action, and whether you believe that creed or follow that guide, no one will doubt but that each has been for the betterment of humanity. The Church of Christ, Scientist, which she established, has grown in less than a half century to one of the great organizations of the world, embracing millions within its membership. Few founders of a sect have witnessed within their own life so great a growth of the organization of which they were the founder. Her death, while regretted, will cause no break in that growth nor take from her followers any of their faith and loyalty to the creed she gave them. One of the wonderful statements she has made was that her followers were to forget personality and work for the cause of Christian Science.

Daily Colonist, Victoria, B.C.

Mrs. Mary Baker Eddy was a remarkable woman. While she was the Founder of what is known as Christian Science, she made no claim to be its originator, for the fundamental Principle of it is as old as the human race. This is not the time to discuss the tenets held by those persons who looked to her as their Leader; but it may not be out of place to express the hope that what is best in her teachings will survive. And there was much that was good in those teachings; more possibly than many of us are prepared to admit. A storm of controversy has raged around Christian Science and Mrs. Eddy. She was the victim of many bitter attacks and much misrepresentation. Shafts of ridicule were discharged against her and those who held as she did; but no one who knows the facts will venture to deny that what she taught has been a source of hope and comfort to thousands.

Calgary Herald, Alberta

With the death of Mary Baker Eddy, one of the most remarkable figures of this or any age passes from the world's stage. To have been for half a century the head of a great movement is a lot conferred on few. To have been for the same length of time the center of heated controversies, of bitter attacks, of religious and philosophical arguments, is a record that few would have survived. To die at the age of ninety, leaving a devoted following that numbers millions of souls, with their churches scattered throughout the world, is but the climax of a wonderful career.

That Mrs. Eddy's death will have any marked effect on the Christian Science church is unlikely. Her work was done. To her, and to her alone, is due the foundation of the faith she taught, and during its earlier history her presence and her personality were no doubt essential to its progress, if not to its very life. In recent years, however, she relegated to others many of her former activities, though she had not altogether retired from work. To-day her church is so fully organized as to be independent even of her personality, and it may be assumed that the machinery of the organization will continue uninterruptedly.

⚜

Republican Picket, Red Lodge, MT

Mary Baker Eddy, Founder of Christian Science, author of a book which has had a phenomenal sale during the last two decades, scholar, teacher, and a genuine Christian, has passed away. Death brought to her no sting, the grave claims no victory. The life of this great and noble woman was as nearly Christlike as that of any person of modern times. Her severest and harshest critics must admit that she was a good woman and that her teachings were not calculated to harm any one. Mrs. Eddy, by her work, her expression of religious thought, her writings, and her life's devotion to the cause she believed to be a just and good cause, attracted the attention of the civilized world, and that world to-day is better because she lived in it. It would be a difficult task to find one who has analyzed the Scriptures as thoroughly as she, and brought them into plainer view, into a clearer light and meaning.

Putting aside all considerations of the healing power said to have been held by this remarkable woman, the plain fact that she taught people how to understand many things in the Bible, which contains so very, very many which the average mind is unable to comprehend — the fact that she accomplished even so much commends her life-work to the earnest, pious consideration of all thinking peoples.

The fact that a mighty army of Christians, intelligent, thinking, practical, conservative men and women in all parts of the world, followed her, respected her, even revered her, should, it seems, be accepted as competent material evidence of the woman's influence for universal good. Unfortunately there is no one to take Mrs. Eddy's place, although the well established, firmly planted church of Christian Science is bound to grow — it is and will continue to be a tremendous force for good.

London Free Press, Ontario

To the long list of women who have been leaders in religious movements of the world, death has added the name of Mary Baker Eddy, Founder of the Christian Science church in America. Born in a farmhouse overlooking the beautiful Merrimac valley, she is described as having been "a very delicate and a very religious little girl." Yet that delicate little girl was destined to become the Founder of a sect which in her own country alone has well on to one hundred thousand communicants, and that has spread all over the world.

There has been a tendency to joke about the teachings of this woman, but a movement that has spread as has Christian Science, including in its ranks men who are leaders in all walks of life, must be viewed as of importance. Particularly is this so when it is considered that it has all been brought to pass in a period of thirty-five years, and that during all of that period the teachings have been criticized and in many quarters strongly denounced.

The world has seen the rise and fall of many new religious movements, but it does not seem as if a better test has ever been devised by man than that which Gamaliel proposed nearly nineteen hundred years ago, when Christianity was first on trial: "If this counsel or this work be of men, it will come to naught; but if it be of God, ye cannot overthrow it."

Madisonian, Virginia City, MT

Mrs. Mary Baker Eddy, Discoverer and Founder of Christian Science, is dead. That announcement carries grief to thousands of people who have been her followers and who have been her pupils throughout the civilized world. There have been scoffers at the belief she taught and the principles she followed, but there are tens of thousands who have benefited by following the lesson of life as she gave it, and there are better men and women to-day than there would have been had she not lived her allotted span of life upon this earth. The world is better for her having lived in it.

Cedar Rapids Evening Times, IA

Mrs. Eddy is the Founder of a society that has its followers in every part of the world. They have gathered themselves together in all the cities of America, and many of the finest edifices for religious purposes have been erected by the Christian Scientists. Whatever some may think of Mrs. Eddy, or of the nature of the influence she has exerted, it must be admitted by all that that influence has been wonderful as well as far-reaching. She touched many of the springs of human activity, and she must have reached the heartstrings of humanity, satisfied some of the quests of the human soul, or she would not have gathered such a world-wide following. It is also to be noted that her followers have not been among the ignorant, but among the great middle class of American intellectual life. Christian Science has flourished most among those classes which are able to think for themselves.

The effect of Mrs. Eddy's death upon the church will not be momentous. That great body is well disciplined, and Mrs. Eddy has provided for the continuation of the organization, as well as she did for its founding. We are told there will be no successor in the church. She will stand alone.

⚜

Butte Tribune-Review, MT

With the passing of Mrs. Eddy, at the age of ninety, the world has lost one of its remarkable women. Her writings and her teachings will continue to live. This truly wonderful woman really commenced the work of her life when the average woman is about to give up. No one can charge that Mrs. Eddy used her great powers to further her own personal interests — and her powers for organization were remarkable. As an observer of human nature she possessed great insight, and had the faculty of gathering around her men and women who carried out her wishes to the letter.

If Mrs. Eddy had accomplished nothing more, she did a great work when she founded *The Christian Science Moni-*

tor, which in a very short space of time has risen to tremendous proportions in the journalistic field. By this alone her influence for good is difficult to estimate. All other things were as nothing compared to her life-work of founding the new thought of Christian Science, and it will not be found wanting in the elevation of the human family to a higher plane. It is now exercising a world-wide influence, and her followers have been recruited from every avenue of life. The most learned and cultured have accepted her teachings, while the humble and unlettered have found comfort therein. Her teachings were the very extreme of some of our other Christian churches, and might be summed up in one word — repose. Her life was a shining example of her own doctrine. No matter from what point of view her life may be judged, her success must be counted as one of the wonders of the age.

Davenport Democrat and Leader, IA

The death of Mary Baker Eddy, Founder of Christian Science, is the most notable event of the past few days. To her followers, she has simply passed on a little way ahead. They declare her presence with them as much as ever, and it is officially announced that she will have no successor as the head of the church.

It is a remarkable career that has closed. In a third of a century the church that she founded has increased until its services draw together weekly the members of more than a thousand churches, and the church is estimated to have a million adherents. There is no more remarkable fact in the past thirty-five years than this, and it was Mrs. Eddy who gave the movement its original inspiration, and who guided it to its present status. Now, say the members of the church, it has become so well established that her going will affect it not at all. "Science" will go on just as if she were still visibly at its head.

Manitowoc Daily Herald, WI

The passing of Mary Baker Eddy, head of the Christian Science church, is an event of more than ordinary moment, and many are the predictions as to the future of the faith which is now professed by over a million people in all lands of the earth. These, and there are many in this city, believe that she has given a real peace message to the world, hope, and ultimate freedom from the ills that flesh is heir to. On the other hand are bitter critics, who deny all her doctrines. The storm of controversy that has raged about Mrs. Eddy and her faith will not cease with her death. It is predicted on one side that the church will topple and fall without the cohesive influence of her captaincy, and on the other that she put the church on its feet long ago and that it will move forward of its own momentum.

Whatever the future of the church — and we are inclined to think that it will flourish and propagate — the tenets Mrs. Eddy preached and taught have had a powerful influence on current thought. Through her, thousands believe they have found the way to health. Whatever it is, there are many, even in Manitowoc, who are sincere in their belief of Science healing and have their own experience to convince the doubting. It should be remembered even by her severest critics that Mrs. Eddy at least taught optimism. Scientists (take those in our midst for example) are sunny, hopeful, and cheerful. The Leader taught that brooding on the ills of life is a sin, and this wholesome doctrine has made chronic grumblers, fretful invalids loaded under a burden of imaginary ills, into bright, active, and better men and women.

Hamilton Times, Ontario

Mrs. Mary Baker Eddy, Founder and Leader of the Christian Science church, is dead, in her ninetieth year. Mrs. Eddy was a remarkable woman, and the influence which she exercised over the hundreds of thousands of her followers makes her a unique figure in religious history. She was more than priestess and prophetess. She was an administrator of great power and capacity, and she possessed to a remarkable degree the gift of dealing with men and women in individuals and in the mass, and winning and retaining their respect and devotion.

Omaha Evening Bee, NE

Contemporaries should not write history, and their attempts at biography should be tentative rather than definite. For this reason no one should undertake to put a final value on the services of Mary Baker Eddy. In many ways she was the most notable woman of her time. It may easily be questioned if any other woman of modern times has wielded the influence and affected directly as many lives as did Mrs. Eddy, and this influence was of the most benign character. It does not matter what individual opinions we may hold as to the correctness of the teachings of Mrs. Eddy. Whether her premise was tenable or her conclusions sound, we are forced to admit that her followers found under her a peace of mind that does not exist elsewhere.

Mrs. Eddy's church brings to its people a message of peace and a promise of better things. It is unobtrusively militant along lines of doing good, and the woman who founded this cult will be followed to her last resting-place by the hearts of millions who looked up to her as the inspired head of a great school of religious activity. She will not be publicly mourned, at least, because her people believe she has gone on to a higher plane of existence, and in this there is no cause for sorrow. She must necessarily be listed among the remarkable women of her time, and the prediction is not unwise that sets down for her a verdict by history that she did good while living.

Des Moines Capital, IA

In reflecting upon the remarkable career which has just terminated at Newton, Massachusetts, the ancient query of Pilate, "What is truth?" seems to come readily to mind. Was Mary Baker Eddy a prophet of God sent into the world to inaugurate a new dispensation? Did she usher in light where only darkness reigned before? Will the church which she founded demonstrate in the years to come that it is builded upon that rock against which the gates of hell can ne'er prevail?

These are questions which have been discussed with growing fervor as the Christian Science propaganda has passed from the day of small things into an era of unmistakable influence in the realm of religious thought. We cannot answer them. The present generation cannot answer them. Regardless of what our individual beliefs, doubts, or intellectual or moral conceptions may be, we are sooner or later forced to the conclusion which Tennyson has so happily expressed, —

> Yet I doubt not through the ages one increasing
> purpose runs,
> And the thoughts of men are widened with the
> process of the suns.

Here we have the philosophy of true growth. Thus does man's horizon broaden as the eyes of his understanding are opened. The quest for truth is rewarded according to our capacity to receive it — in the fulness of time.

Ft. Wayne Sentinel, IN

Mrs. Mary Baker Eddy, Founder of the Christian Science church, leaves behind her such a monument of achievement as no woman in any age, perhaps, had builded. The Christian Science church and its propaganda in a matter of some thirty years have gone almost literally around the world. To-day in the United States there is hardly a community of notable size that has not an organized body of this sect, and doubtless none that has not one or more who have accepted and practised its doctrines. What the future of the church is to be, without its Founder and Leader, only time can tell; but it is true that to-day the Christian Science denomination shows such a spread over the earth and such proportions of growth as have been true of no other religious movement in like time in any age of the world. Millions of people acknowledge the doctrines formulated and spread by Mrs. Eddy and her followers. The movement has built magnificent cathedrals and churches, it has established centers for its literature all over the globe, it has enlisted men and women of the highest type of intellect in its teachings and in its propaganda.

This is the work of a woman whose nature was timid, whose disposition was modest, and whose tastes were retiring. Mrs. Eddy never sought the limelight. Where she might have made herself heroic, she was content to live as much out of sight as possible, and watch and direct the growth of the sect she had founded and the doctrine she had enunciated.

❧

Pioneer, Bemidji, MN

With no thought as to the right or wrong of the religious organization of which Mrs. Eddy was at the head, this much can be said: This Boston woman's life was as beautiful as it was devoted, and as sublime as were her teachings. Her church, the Church of Christ, Scientist, or as it is more commonly known, Christian Scientist, sprang from the mind of Mrs. Eddy. Her theory has been so convincing that men and women of culture and master minds in all corners of civilization have adopted it as the true doctrine — modern edifices in hundreds of cities bearing evidence of this fact.

The Christian Scientists publish a modern and, be it said to their credit, remarkably clean daily newspaper in addition to many other publications. The growth of the church has been phenomenal.

✠

Ames Intelligencer, IA

In the passing of Mrs. Eddy the world will learn more of Christian Science and have a higher conception of the teachings of the grand, good woman who put sunshine into thousands of gloomy homes. Mrs. Eddy, as the world knows her, is dead, but for the followers of Christian Science and all enlightened Christian churches she still lives and will continue to live.

✠

Hastings Daily Tribune, NE

Unquestionably Mrs. Eddy was the most remarkable woman of her day, as she founded a religion the influence of which is being felt around the world, and it gains in strength as it gains in age.

Rock Island Union, IL

The life of Mary Baker Eddy has come to a close. She was no ordinary person. Whatever may be your belief, or whether you make any religious professions or not, you must admit that she has accomplished great things, and her accomplishments have resulted in good. The facts — the proof of these two propositions — are apparent to all. Christian Science was "discovered" by her. She was its fountainhead, and to-day, thirty-one years after the first church was chartered, there are over a million adherents. That is proof sufficient of the first statement. The hundreds of men and women that are known by you, who have become better, morally and physically, after becoming adherents of that faith, is ample proof of the second proposition.

The life of Mary Baker Eddy was a wonderful life. The story of her struggles is filled with the power of will — at least will — over matter. Here was a master mind. It was wonderful to conceive and to carry into execution a conception so broad and of such magnitude. It was wonderful that she was able to resist the temptations, the flatteries of fawning sycophants, and adhere to the one great theme, the power "of the infinite over the finite," the "elimination of wrong" by the establishment — the eternal prevalence — of right.

Then there comes the third proposition, which also must be admitted by all. Christian Science has come to stay, and its growth for the future, if predictions may be based upon what it has done in the past, will be of considerable magnitude. Mrs. Eddy had found a place in the religious world that was not being filled, and an enduring fame has been established.

※

Portland Journal, OR

Mrs. Eddy was a wonderful woman. None but a wonderful woman could have founded an organization which placed her at the head of more than a million followers. They are followers in a sense that means far more than the ordinary relation between leader and disciple. It involves a consecration of faith and life, the absolute change in personal conduct, a complete reordering of daily life, and the investment of huge sums in buildings and activities related to the Science life. History reveals no other woman who has by personal force exercised such power. As Founder of the Science church Mrs. Eddy rose into position by personal achievement, and through the growth, spread, and perpetuity of the organization will have an enduring fame.

Every faith or creed has its opponents and critics, and Christian Science has its share. Many of us are not ready to go to the extreme length of faith that it involves, but we can all agree that the talents and achievements of its Founder are entitled to a wholesome respect.

Anderson Herald, IN

There are many who do not subscribe to the Christian Science doctrine, but there are few who do not realize that in the death of Mrs. Eddy one of the greatest women of this or any other generation has gone. Barring all reference to the value of her creed, and most people whether they subscribe to it or not will admit its great value, it is enough to know that in the space of one life she has created one of the great religious institutions of the period and counts her followers by the hundreds of thousands. Her influence on her own generation was great and all for good. It is more than possible that it will extend, through her books and disciples, to many generations to come, and be one of the great factors in the development of humanity.

Malden Evening News, MA

Mrs. Eddy brought happiness to thousands of people. Whether they are imagining that happiness, or whether it will be temporary or lasting, is begging the question. Through her writings and the creed she founded, people weary in body and soul and mind have found rest when they could not find it elsewhere. Therein she did a vast amount of good. Humanity is decidedly her debtor. There is no question about her being the most wonderful woman of her day and generation. She won the faith of thousands of intelligent people, and they found in that faith what they had been groping about for in medicine and other religions. That was enough for them, and the best endorsement she could have secured.

Pacific Commercial Advertiser, Honolulu, HI

Whatever may be one's religious views, it will be generally recognized that one of the great women of the world has passed away in the death of Mary Baker Eddy. That one person, and that person a woman, should have, practically through her individual efforts, built up an organization as solid and as deeply rooted as the Christian Science church, stamps such a person as great, in every sense of the word.

Jackson Daily News, MS

Regardless of conflicting opinions concerning this new religious cult, the cold facts of history must be conceded. Mrs. Eddy enlisted under her banner nearly a million followers within a decade, and she must be accorded a unique place among the religious leaders and thinkers of this day and generation. The Christian Science movement has grown so rapidly and shown so much virility amid unusual storm and stress, that it may be expected to survive the death of its Leader, and continue to show strength and vitality among the creeds and cults of the day. Even here in Mississippi, where the people are slow to adopt new spiritual ideas, clinging tenaciously to the orthodox faith of their fathers, Christian Science has obtained a strong foothold.

Credit must be given where credit is due, regardless of your personal views. In summarizing the life of Mrs. Eddy, therefore, we must admit that a woman with the will and power to establish, within little more than ten years, a new religious cult, and place it upon such a firm foundation, must possess more than ordinary powers. The growth of the Christian Science movement, the establishment of its churches in magnificent buildings, and the organization of hundreds of thousands of people in a faith which has become world-wide, — this has been one of the extraordinary phenomena of the present and the past centuries.

❧

Daily Traveler, Arkansas City, KS

Mrs. Eddy was a great and grand woman. We believe her to have been the greatest woman the world ever knew. She was the most loved and at the same time the most maligned woman of the age.

She gave to the world a religion that will be found eternal. Those who have espoused it have found it a great solace and it has made them better citizens. Its teachings have brought a good God closer to them and caused them to know that He is "a very present help." It teaches that God is Spirit, Life, Truth, and Love, and that "man is His image and likeness," and that the real man and the universe are spiritual, not material. It teaches that God is the only cause and creator, and there is no other presence or power. Upon these principles is founded the religion which Mrs. Eddy discovered and gave to the world, and it is rapidly covering the face of the earth.

To Christian Scientists Mrs. Eddy was their beloved

Leader. She was their wayshower to an ever-present salvation. They feel that her life-work was finished and that she has left a wonderful heritage to those who desire to accept it.

✻

Meriden Record, CT

The passing of Mary Baker Eddy removes one of the most remarkable women of the present century. It matters little whether one subscribes to her creed or not, the fact remains that this woman became a potent factor in making people think and in compelling them to blaze the way either for her beliefs or for others for which they themselves discovered.

There are many people who have no sympathy with Christian Science who have indirectly been greatly aided by the interest taken in it. All the theories of mental science, the effect of mind over matter, gained new impetus from Mrs. Eddy's teachings. The very extremes to which she went caused people to look up the subject, if for no loftier purpose than that of curiosity. Investigation led into devious ways. The result was a large addition to the sum total of human knowledge. And it must be admitted that if the general results of the knowledge gained by investigations made into the subject of Christian Science could be known, it would be found it had been for the good of humanity.

East Oregonian, Pendleton, OR

It is estimated that in the United States there are one million people who uphold the Christian Science creed — a creed that was first promulgated by Mrs. Mary Baker Eddy. For the most part they are earnest and cultured people. Without ostentation they worship God in accordance with their beliefs. Their interpretation of the gospel is somewhat different from the orthodox version, and this has brought forth criticism from those who follow the old-time faiths. Whether the Christian Scientists are at fault and their critics are right, or whether just the opposite is true, is an open question. If the Christian Science church is founded upon error, it cannot live; but the fact that the church has lived this long, and has grown in popularity until it now has a million followers, indicates strongly that there is much truth in the teachings of the departed Founder and Leader.

Jackson Clarion-Ledger, MS

The death of this famed woman removes one of the most prominent characters of the present century. However one may feel disposed to criticize the religious faith founded by her, all must admit that she was a most marvelous woman, whose life was devoted to the uplift of mankind. That she was possessed of an intellect far above the average cannot be denied, neither can it be questioned that she used all of her ability in her efforts toward the good of humanity. The world's highest meed of praise is bestowed upon those who have made the greatest efforts toward its good, and it is this fact that has assured for her a high place in the estimation of the world.

The preponderance in public thought which she attained as the Discoverer and Founder of the doctrine of Christian Science, and the tender mother love which finds a place for her in thousands of hearts, is a tribute to her unselfish love for her fellow-man.

Chicago Journal

The death of Mary Baker Eddy well might serve as inspiration for a new beatitude: Blessed are they who need no monument; their names are graven on many hearts. Opinions may differ as to the adequacy of the Christian Science faith to answer the full requirements of the human soul; but few deny that to hundreds of thousands of devoted followers the teachings of Mrs. Eddy have been a hope and inspiration.

Wisely anticipating the time when she could be with her followers only in spirit, she recently had withdrawn herself as far as possible from the details of church management. Consequently, the organization that she has perfected will continue to perform its functions. Her life-work was well completed and will endure.

Montreal Gazette

Of the many women who have led religious movements in modern times, none attracted more attention or established a wider influence than Mrs. Mary Baker Eddy, who died at her home near Boston on Saturday night. Mrs. Eddy's followers or fellow-believers were not generally of the class that is subject to emotional excitement. They were largely of superior intelligence, readers, and always ready and able to defend the doctrines they accepted. They maintain in Boston a daily paper, which in its breadth of views and ability to discuss large questions has few superiors in America. The Christian Science people have been scoffed at and laughed at, and some of them, going to extremes, have suffered harder fortune. Their story, like the story of many another religious movement, may, more than anything else, mean that the human heart longs for the preaching of faith, and turns to whoever can preach it with earnestness and sincerity.

Grand Rapids Evening Press, MI

If history makes clear any one fact, it is that contemporaneous judgments are often inaccurate. The perspective of time is necessary to a calm analysis of the influences which shape thought. Posterity more than once has rejected those acclaimed prophets in a bygone day and crowned those who were overlooked by their fellows.

The axiom will hold good in the case of Mrs. Mary Baker Eddy, Discoverer and Founder of Christian Science, who died Saturday evening. The world is too close to her life and her work to give an unbiased decision as to their significance. On the one hand are her thousands of followers, scattered in almost every civilized land, who believe she has given to the world a real message of peace, hope, and ultimate freedom from the ills to which flesh so long has been heir. On the other hand are her many critics, some bitter, some mild, but all denying her doctrines.

Whatever the future has to tell of Mrs. Eddy and her teaching, and aside from whatever opinion one may have as to the tenets she preached, it is certain that she has been a powerful factor in current thought. The growth of Christian Science as the sincere belief of men and women of varied classes, the hundreds of magnificent churches which have been reared by her disciples, and, most of all, the enormous circulation of her book, *Science and Health with Key to the Scriptures,* proves that. Through Mrs. Eddy thousands believe they found the way to health.

If any one influence which she exerted should be remembered, it is that she taught optimism. Christian Scientists are sunny, hopeful, cheerful. The Leader taught that brooding on the ills of life is a sin, and this wholesome doctrine has remade chronic grumblers and fretful invalids, loaded under a burden of imaginary ills, into bright, active, and helpful men and women.

Cleveland Plain Dealer

The death of the Founder of Christian Science removes from the world one of the most remarkable women of all time. Her career commands admiration, no matter what opinion may be held of her teachings. Mrs. Eddy founded a religious sect that during her lifetime multiplied its proselytes till it has become a great force in American life. She retained her position as sole Leader, and was looked up to by her followers as the sole source of inspiration. Virile and vigorous, she was a natural commander, a natural organizer, a woman who displayed intellectual qualities of the highest order. The work that Mrs. Eddy has done will remain as her monument. Christian Science will not perish with the death of its Founder. It has assumed proportions that assure permanency.

Baltimore Sun, MD

Mrs. Mary Baker Eddy, Founder of Christian Science and author of many books treating upon that subject, is dead at Boston, having some months ago passed into her ninetieth year. Mrs. Eddy was one of the remarkable women of her time. A sickly, weak child, she grew into a frail woman who seemed to have but a slender hold on existence, and yet she lived to an unusual age, a life full of work and teeming with results. Establishing a church, she remained its head to the time of her demise, managing its affairs with great executive ability and penetrating judgment. Whatever may be the fate of the church she founded, now that her forceful hand is removed from the management of its affairs, there can be no doubt of her wonderful administrative ability, her keen insight into human nature, and her tremendous capacity for work. Her place in history as one of the really extraordinary women of her day is secure.

For Mrs. Eddy:
City Government Passes Resolutions of Respect

Concord Monitor, NH

AT THE meeting of the city government, Monday night [Dec. 26], action was taken on the death of the Rev. Mary Baker Eddy by the passage of appropriate resolutions. The resolutions were introduced by Alderman Cressy, and in presenting them he said:

"The year 1910 is soon to be a thing of the past, so is this city charter and this city government, and before the book of records which has been so faithfully kept by our worthy city clerk is closed, it seems wise, though a regrettable duty, to have spread thereon this resolution which I am about to introduce over the death of one of Concord's most distinguished citizens, the Rev. Mary Baker Eddy.

"Although some two years ago Mrs. Eddy took up a temporary residence in Massachusetts, that she might be nearer her work, Concord proudly and justly claims Mrs. Eddy as one of her citizens, and in her death we lose an honored, respected, and beloved benefactor. While some may differ in their technical belief, all Concord bows its head reverently at Mrs. Eddy's death, and I ask your careful consideration of the following resolution:

"By the decease of the Rev. Mary Baker Eddy, Concord loses its most distinguished citizen. During the many years she resided here, thousands of people from our own land and from foreign countries have visited our city in paying their respects to her. Through her followers, Concord has become known through the civilized world.

"Mrs. Eddy was distinguished by public spirit, deep generosity, wide charity, and tender and thoughtful helpfulness, and it seems fitting and appropriate that we, the mayor and the board of aldermen and the common council of the city of Concord, take some action in behalf of our citizens to express our appreciation of her residence among us and our esteem of her character; therefore

"Be it resolved, that by the death of the Rev. Mary Baker Eddy the world has suffered an irreparable loss and the citizens of Concord the loss of an honored and a devoted friend of our city, whose motto was 'to injure no man, but to bless all mankind.' "*

---

*The First Church of Christ, Scientist, and Miscellany, page 353.

Index